KIDS Draw

BIG

BOOK OF

EVERYTHING

MANGA

KIDS Draw BIG BOOK OF EVERYTHING MANGA

CHRISTOPHER HART

WATSON-GUPTILL PUBLICATIONS/NEW YORK

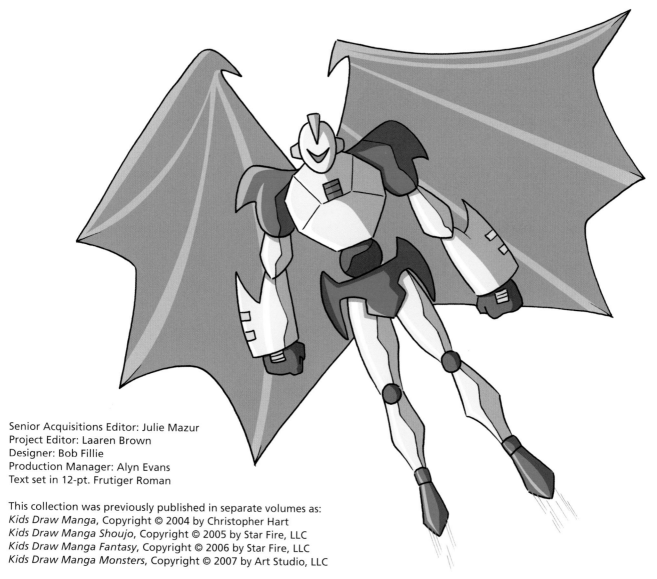

Senior Acquisitions Editor: Julie Mazur
Project Editor: Laaren Brown
Designer: Bob Fillie
Production Manager: Alyn Evans
Text set in 12-pt. Frutiger Roman

This collection was previously published in separate volumes as:
Kids Draw Manga, Copyright © 2004 by Christopher Hart
Kids Draw Manga Shoujo, Copyright © 2005 by Star Fire, LLC
Kids Draw Manga Fantasy, Copyright © 2006 by Star Fire, LLC
Kids Draw Manga Monsters, Copyright © 2007 by Art Studio, LLC

The 2009 edition is published by Watson-Guptill Publications,
an imprint of the Crown Publishing Group,
a division of Random House, Inc., New York.
www.crownpublishing.com
www.watsonguptill.com

Library of Congress Catalogue-in-Publication Data
The CIP data for this title may be obtained from the Library of Congress
Library of Congress Card Number: 2008933747

ISBN: 978-0-8230-9509-4

Printed in China

First printing, 2009

VISIT US AT
www.kidsdraw.com

CONTENTS

INTRODUCTION 7

KIDS DRAW MANGA 8

Manga Basics 10

Cool Manga Characters 24

The Battling Robots of Japanese Comics! 48

Bonus Pages: Advanced Drawings 56

KIDS DRAW MANGA MONSTERS 68

Monster Basics 70

Manga Monster Characters 84

KIDS DRAW MANGA SHOUJO 128

Shoujo Basics 130

School Comics 152

Magic Time 164

Fairies and Friends 182

KIDS DRAW MANGA FANTASY 188

Manga Fantasy Basics 190

Fairies and Knights 202

Flying Characters 216

Magical Effects! 224

Supernatural Beings 234

NOW IT'S YOUR TURN! 248

INDEX 253

INTRODUCTION

Welcome to the world of manga! "Manga" is a Japanese word that means "comics." We use it to describe Japanese-style comics. You can recognize most manga characters by their big, shiny eyes. If you bought this book, you probably know that manga is a huge craze with kids and teens. This book will teach you to create manga drawings so cool, your friends will be begging to learn how you did them!

The first section, *Kids Draw Manga*, starts with the basics, like how to draw manga-style faces and heads. Then you'll learn to draw a bunch of manga-style characters, from young boys and girls to intense sci-fi commanders and giant fighting robots.

The second section, *Kids Draw Manga Monsters*, shows you step-by-step how to draw all kinds of fun manga monsters, from little furballs to giant dinosaur types. These monsters are sometimes mischievous, sometimes cute, or maybe even evil. Regardless of their traits, they all have two things in common: (1) they have a lot of personality and (2) they lack the ability to frighten anyone—especially the characters in the next section.

"Shoujo" manga is perhaps the best-loved style of manga, featuring stories of adventure, friendship, loyalty, and teamwork. In the third section, *Kids Draw Manga Shoujo*, you'll find leading men and fantasy fighters, fashionable teens, school kids, "magical girls," goddesses, demi-gods, and even more knights and fairies. You'll learn to create these classic characters with your own special touches.

We'll end with the magical world of *Kids Draw Manga Fantasy*. You'll learn to draw magical fairies, beautiful princesses, mermaids, wizards and warlocks, demon beasts, futuristic knights, and many more supernatural creatures. Along the way, you'll learn to create super-cool effects and get secret tips to make your drawings sparkle.

Every drawing is broken down into steps that are easy to follow, and each section starts with simple characters, then moves on to more complicated ones—this way, the book grows with you as you learn. If you're a manga fan and you like to draw, get ready for hours and hours of creative fun!

Manga Basics 10

DRAWING THE EYE
DRAWING THE MOUTH
DRAWING THE NOSE
THE SHAPE OF THE HEAD
TIPS AND TRICKS
DRAWING THE BODY: BOYS VERSUS GIRLS

DIVIDING THE BODY INTO SECTIONS
BASIC POSES
MORE TIPS AND TRICKS
FLYING POSES
PUNCHING POSE
KICKING POSE

Cool Manga Characters 24

BASIC MANGA BOY
BASIC MANGA GIRL
POINTY-HAIRED GUY
WORRIED BOY
SCHOOLGIRL
FUNNY RUNNER
CRABBY CATHY
MANGA PRINCESS
CASUAL TEEN

WARRIOR PRINCESS
TEENAGE DEFENDER
MANGA BUSINESS EXECUTIVE
MYSTERIOUS SWORDSMAN
HOMEWORK TROUBLE
HERO KNIGHT
LASER BLAST
LEADER OF THE EARTH REBELS
MAGIC SORCERESS

The Battling Robots of Japanese Comics! 48

MR. COLOSSUS
USING ARMS AS WEAPONS

FLYING ROBOT SOLDIER
LASER FIGHTER

Bonus Pages: Advanced Drawings 56

EXTREME PERSPECTIVE
STYLISH TEEN
DARK MAGIC

SPACESHIP COMMANDER
PLAY BALL!
GALAXY SHIP PILOT

MANGA BASICS

Let's get right to the good stuff! Take out a pencil and paper, and let's get started.

Drawing the Eye

The eyes are the most important part of any manga character. Draw them very big and round, with huge shines. There are at least two shines in the typical manga-style eye, sometimes even more.

BOY'S EYE

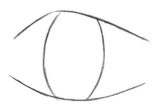

1. Draw the top eyelid.

2. Add the iris (the colored part of the eye).

3. Draw the bottom eyelid.

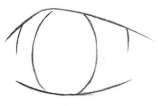

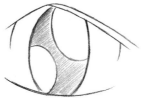

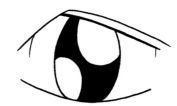

4. Show the inner and outer edges of the eye.

5. Add the upper eyelid crease and the "shines." Color in the iris.

6. Darken the iris. Leave the shines white.

GIRL'S EYE

Girls' eyes are drawn differently from boys' eyes. Most girls' eyes are drawn in the shape of a box.

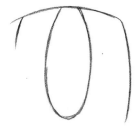

1. Start the outline of the eye. Add the iris.

2. Draw the bottom of the eye.

3. Draw the eyelashes.

4. Add the "shines" inside the iris.

5. Color in the eyelashes and the iris. Leave the shines white.

Now that you've seen how to draw the eye by itself, try adding a pair of eyes to a real manga face. Trace the head in step 1, then follow the other steps to add the eyes.

1.

2.

3.

4.

5.

6.

Drawing the Mouth

Look at all of the different expressions you can create, just by changing the shape of the mouth. Here are a few typical mouth positions and some tips on drawing them.

DISAPPOINTED
Draw a small, down-turned line and place it a little off center.

SURPRISED
Use a medium circle.

HAPPY
Draw a smile. Place it closer to the nose than to the chin.

REALLY HAPPY
Draw a wide mouth, usually without any tongue.

SHOCKED
Draw a wide mouth—so wide, in fact, that you can't even see the lower lip!

CONFUSED
A mini "o" does the trick!

Drawing the Nose

Manga characters have sharp noses that turn up at the end. Notice that as the head turns, the nose looks like it's changing shape. Here are a few rules to remember so you'll always get the nose right.

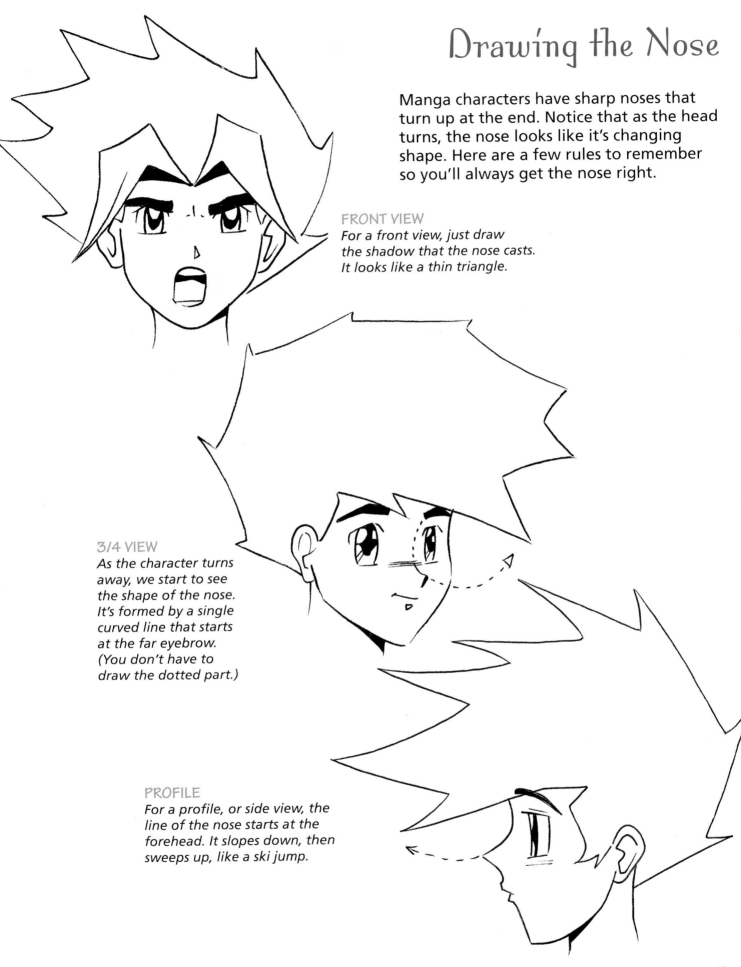

FRONT VIEW
For a front view, just draw the shadow that the nose casts. It looks like a thin triangle.

3/4 VIEW
As the character turns away, we start to see the shape of the nose. It's formed by a single curved line that starts at the far eyebrow. (You don't have to draw the dotted part.)

PROFILE
For a profile, or side view, the line of the nose starts at the forehead. It slopes down, then sweeps up, like a ski jump.

The Shape of the Head

Okay, so you've learned how to draw the eyes, nose, and mouth. Now you need a place to put them! Our next job is to tackle the overall shape of the manga-style head. Most manga heads have certain things in common.

BOY'S HEAD

Let's start with a typical manga boy's head. This one is a 3/4 view, which is halfway between a front view and a side view.

The face begins to curve in at the eyebrow.

The face begins to curve out at the cheek, just above the tip of the nose.

The neck attaches to the back of the skull (not to the bottom of the ear, as you might think!).

GIRL'S HEAD

Here is a front view of a typical girl. In manga, girls have very big hairstyles that make their heads look taller.

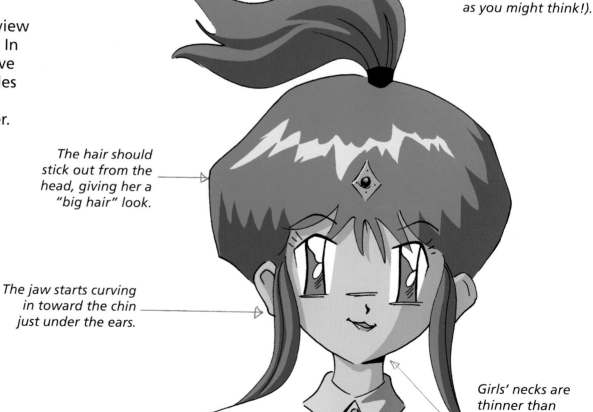

The hair should stick out from the head, giving her a "big hair" look.

The jaw starts curving in toward the chin just under the ears.

Girls' necks are thinner than boys' necks.

Here are some tips that will help your drawings look professional.

In a 3/4 view, the chin slopes back at a severe angle. Manga characters almost never have chins that stick out.

In a front view, the tip of the chin is pointy, not round.

The ears are placed low on the head.

The top of the head is always large. This helps make the character look young.

Drawing the Body: Boys Versus Girls

Manga boys are usually drawn taller than manga girls.
Also, the boy's upper body is straight, while the girl's
upper body changes shape. The girl's body is wide at
the shoulders, narrow at the waist, and wide at the
hips. The girl's shoulders are usually wider than her
waist, which helps make her look young.

Dividing the Body into Sections

These drawings show you how to break the body into sections. This will help you draw more realistic poses.

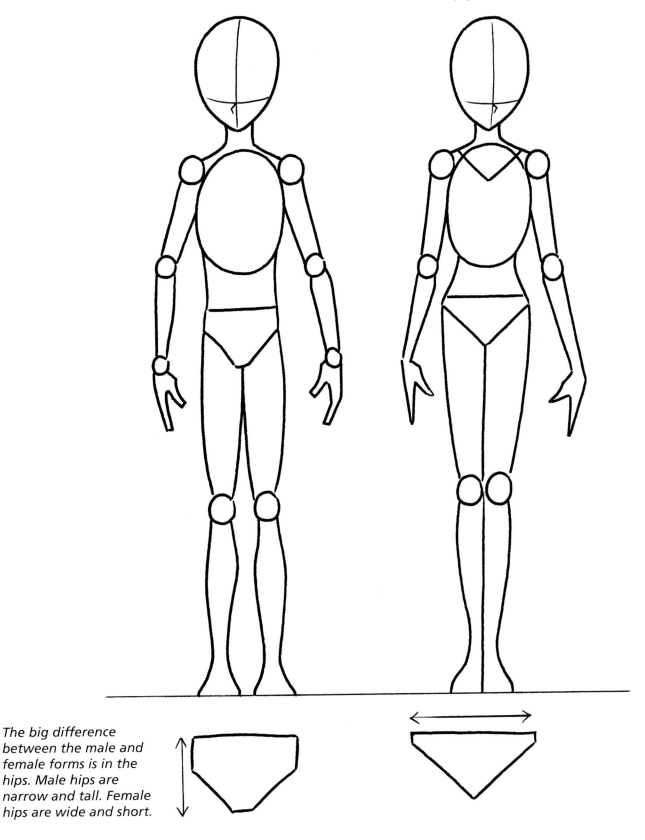

The big difference between the male and female forms is in the hips. Male hips are narrow and tall. Female hips are wide and short.

Basic Poses

Take a paper and pencil, and try sketching some of the poses on this page. *Sketching* means drawing quickly, without worrying about the details. Just try to capture the feeling of each pose. This is great practice for drawing the cool manga characters coming up in just a few pages!

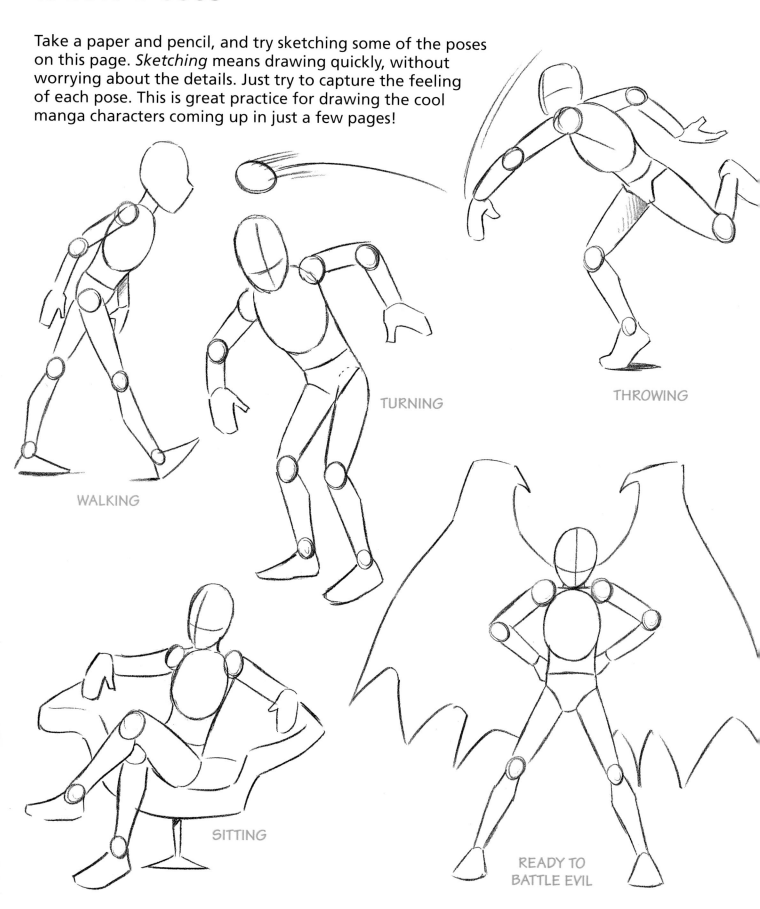

WALKING

TURNING

THROWING

SITTING

READY TO BATTLE EVIL

More Tips and Tricks

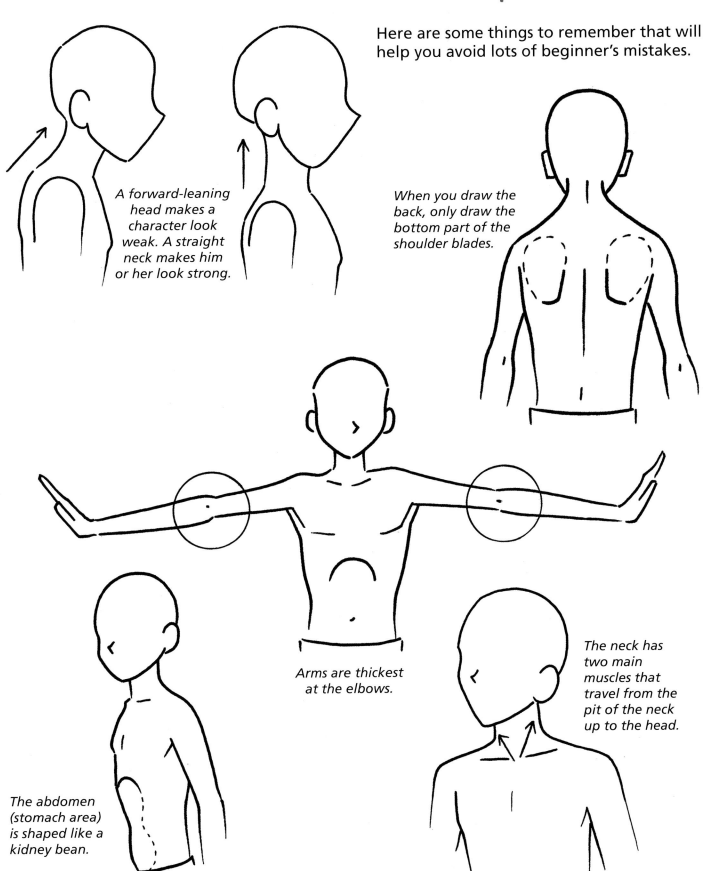

A forward-leaning head makes a character look weak. A straight neck makes him or her look strong.

When you draw the back, only draw the bottom part of the shoulder blades.

Arms are thickest at the elbows.

The abdomen (stomach area) is shaped like a kidney bean.

The neck has two main muscles that travel from the pit of the neck up to the head.

Flying Poses

It's fun to watch manga gals and guys zoom through the sky. But if you don't choose just the right position, it can look like your character is falling instead of flying. Here are some sure-fire poses to create a sense of flight. Give 'em a try!

FRONT POSE, ARMS DOWN

This pose only works if the head is tilted up. If she were looking straight at us, it would seem as though she were standing still instead of flying.

In all flying poses, it's important to add little streaks, called "speed lines." They create a feeling of movement.

SIDE POSE, ONE ARM FORWARD

Place one arm stretched out straight in front of the character and the other arm back. This is a classic flying pose. Make sure the hair looks like it's being blown by the wind.

STRAIGHT-ON POSE, ARMS OUTSTRETCHED

In this pose, we shouldn't be able to see the legs or feet at all.

Punching Pose

Whenever one person punches
another person, both figures
must move in the same direction.
It's as important to show the
reaction to the punch as it is
to show the punch itself!

Kicking Pose

Just as with the punch,
both figures should move
in the same direction.

COOL MANGA CHARACTERS

 inally, the part you've been waiting for! Now that you've learned the basics, it's time to draw a ton of cool, original manga characters!

Basic Manga Boy

Like all manga characters, this boy has a wide face and a pointy chin.

1. Start with a circle for the top of the head. It's easier to build onto a simple shape than to draw the entire head from scratch.

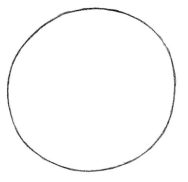

2. Add the chin.

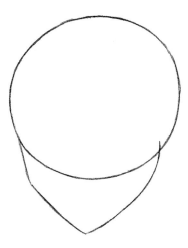

3. Put some guidelines on the face. These are lines that artists use to help them put the features on the face. They also show which way the head is facing.

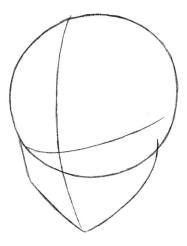

4. Place the facial features on the guidelines. The eyes go on the horizontal guideline. The bridge of the nose goes on the vertical guideline. The mouth is drawn off-center. Make the eyebrows bold. Place the ear where the jaw and the top of the head meet.

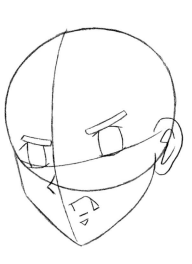

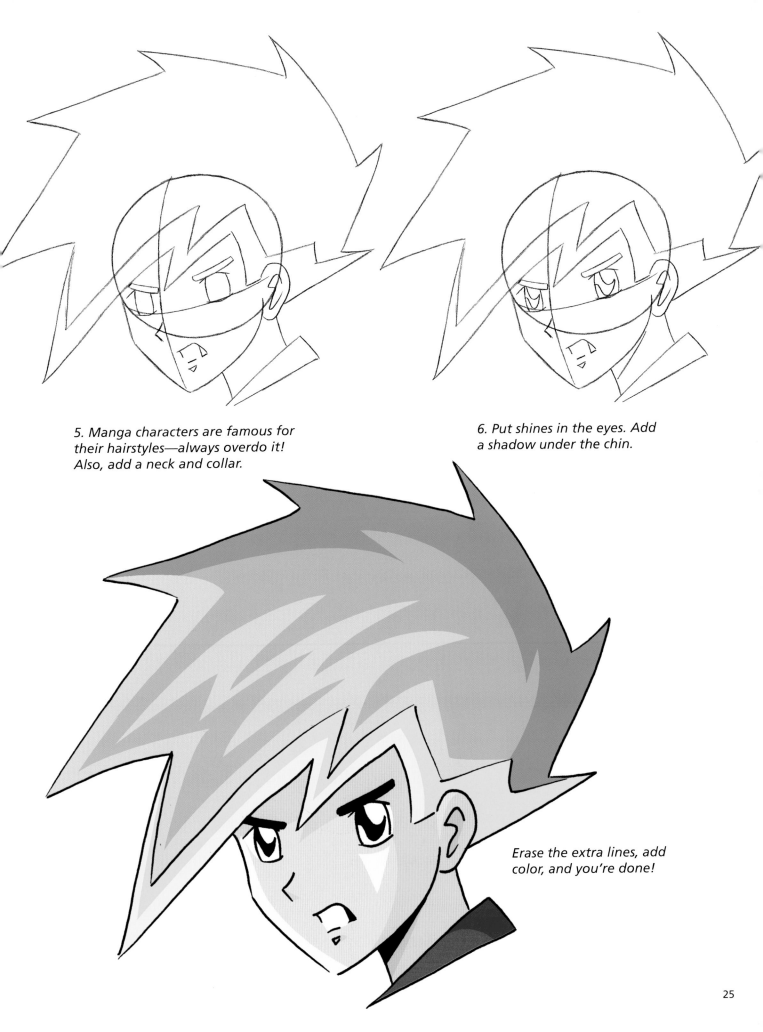

5. Manga characters are famous for their hairstyles—always overdo it! Also, add a neck and collar.

6. Put shines in the eyes. Add a shadow under the chin.

Erase the extra lines, add color, and you're done!

Basic Manga Girl

Now let's do the same basic pose, but for a girl.

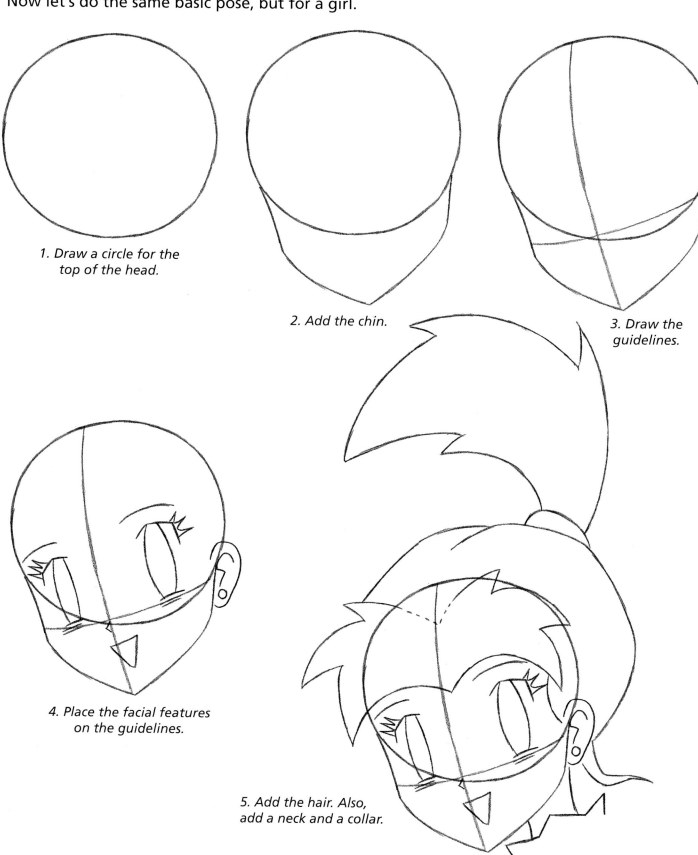

1. Draw a circle for the top of the head.

2. Add the chin.

3. Draw the guidelines.

4. Place the facial features on the guidelines.

5. Add the hair. Also, add a neck and a collar.

6. Put shines in the eyes. Add a shadow just below the chin.

7. Erase the extra lines, add color, and that's it!

Pointy-Haired Guy

Here's another basic manga boy. Since you know the basics by now, I'll use fewer steps.

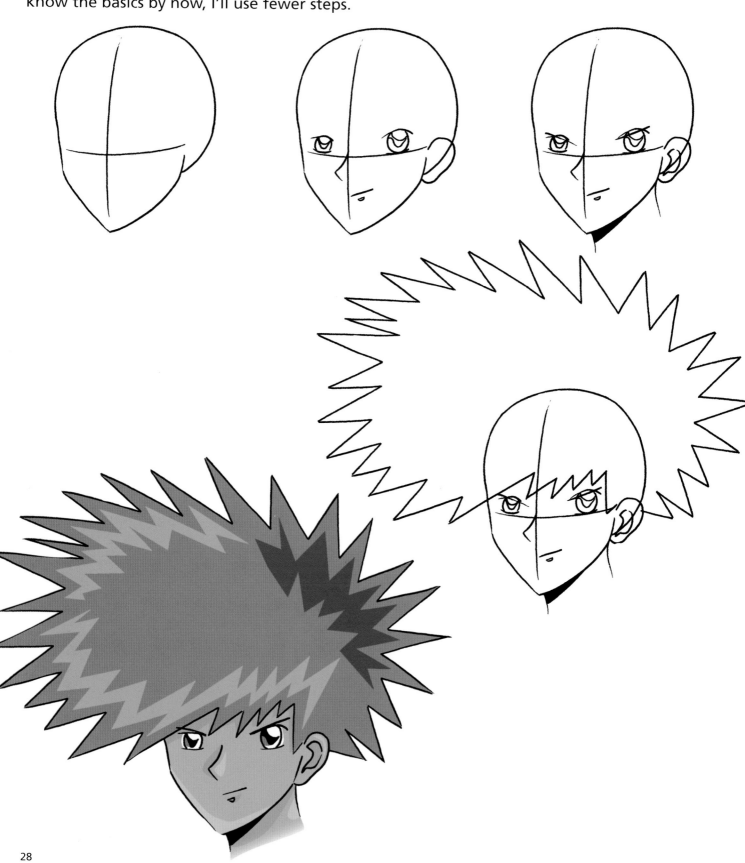

Worried Boy

This character has interesting eyes and a different hairstyle. But notice that he still has the same basic manga style: big head and pointy chin.

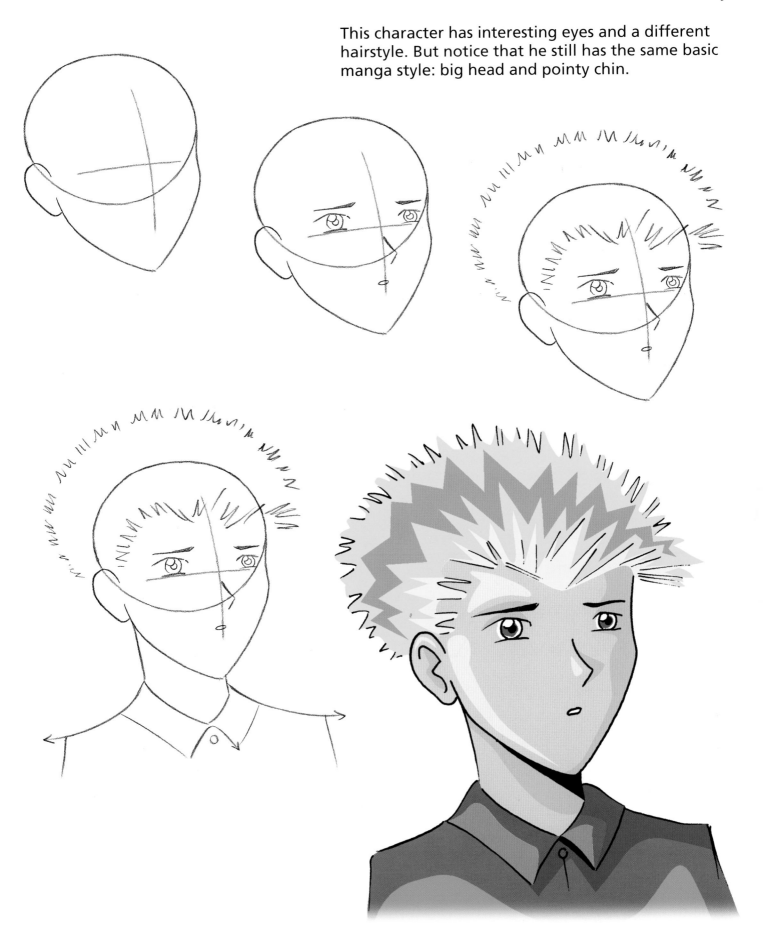

Schoolgirl

Here's a figure for you to try. As with all drawings, concentrate on the big shapes first and save the details for last.

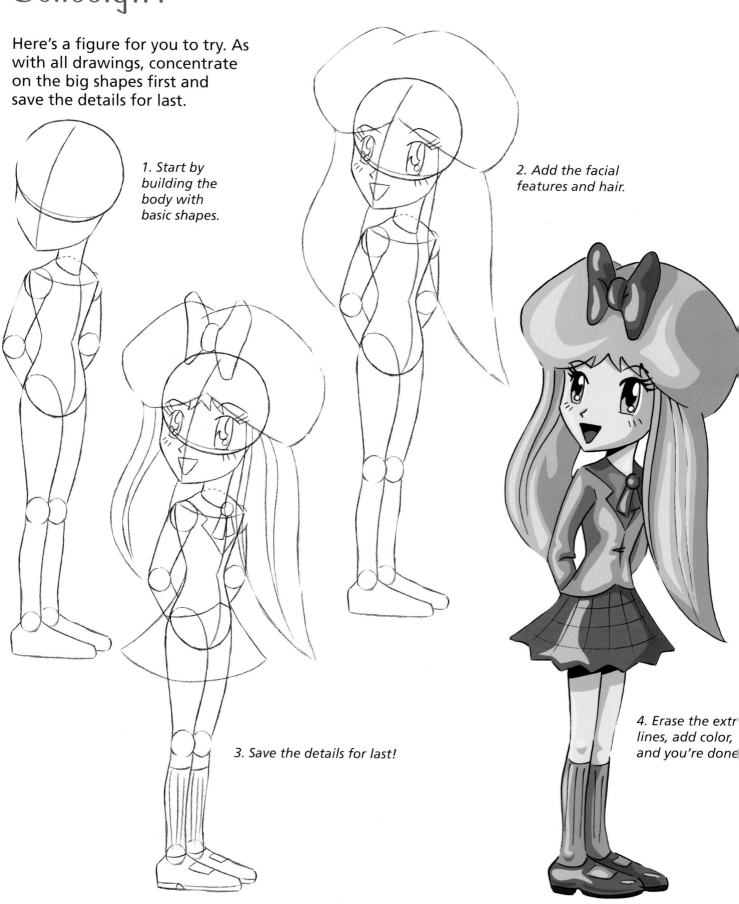

1. Start by building the body with basic shapes.

2. Add the facial features and hair.

3. Save the details for last!

4. Erase the extra lines, add color, and you're done

Funny Runner

Most people lean forward when they run. To draw a goofy run, make your character lean back, chest out, with both arms behind. Don't let either foot touch the ground. The shadow below him is a nice touch—it tells people where the ground is.

Crabby Cathy

What a grouch! I can easily imagine this girl as somebody's mean older sister. Those upturned braids are prickly reminders of her personality. And her arm position, called "arms akimbo," shows her to be quite demanding.

Casual Teen

Teenage Defender

Teens play an important role in manga—they save the world! It's hard to do battle with only a candy bar and a baseball glove, so manga artists often give their characters a little help, like this laser blaster.

Manga Business Executive

She's a power broker in the corporate world. She wears a stylish suit, but nothing too flashy. High heels, jazzy earrings, and buttons on the sleeve complete her style.

Mysterious Swordsman

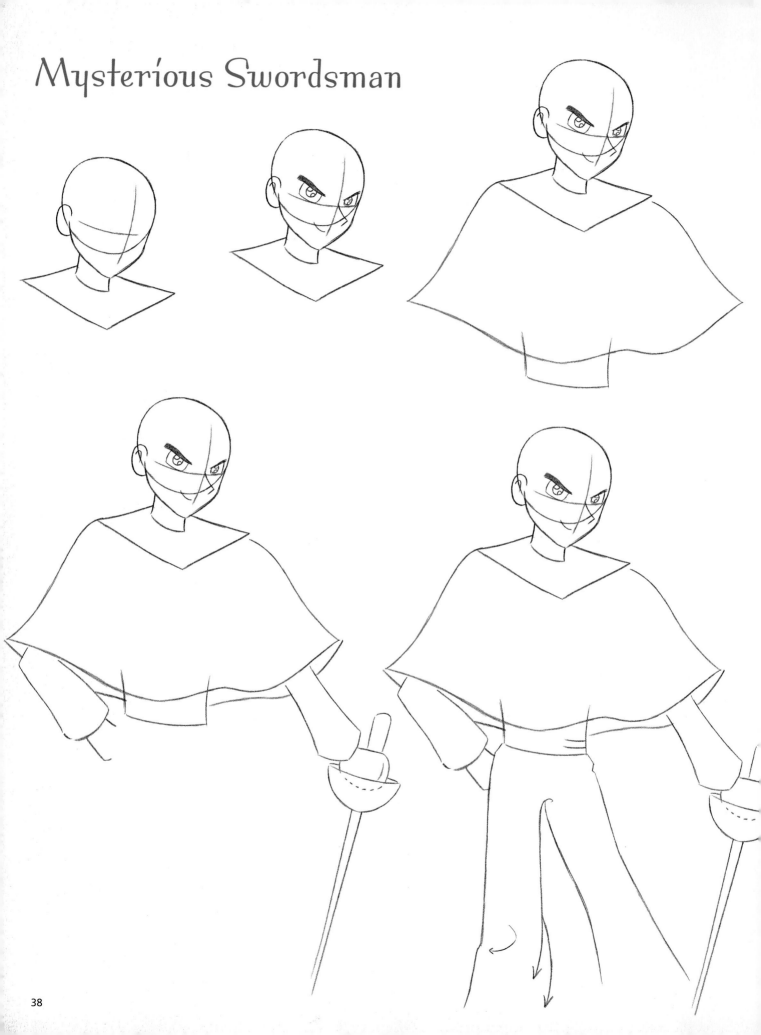

Homework Trouble

This poor girl can't figure out her class assignment, and her kitty can't figure out what's bothering her. I've broken the drawing down into lots of steps to help you.

Hero Knight

I've given this knight windblown hair to make him look more dramatic. Make sure all of the hair blows in the same direction or it will look strange. His heavy sword tells us that he must be strong, as do his extra-wide shoulders.

Laser Blast

Try to be creative with your special effects! You can draw lasers as streams, waves, or even pellets.

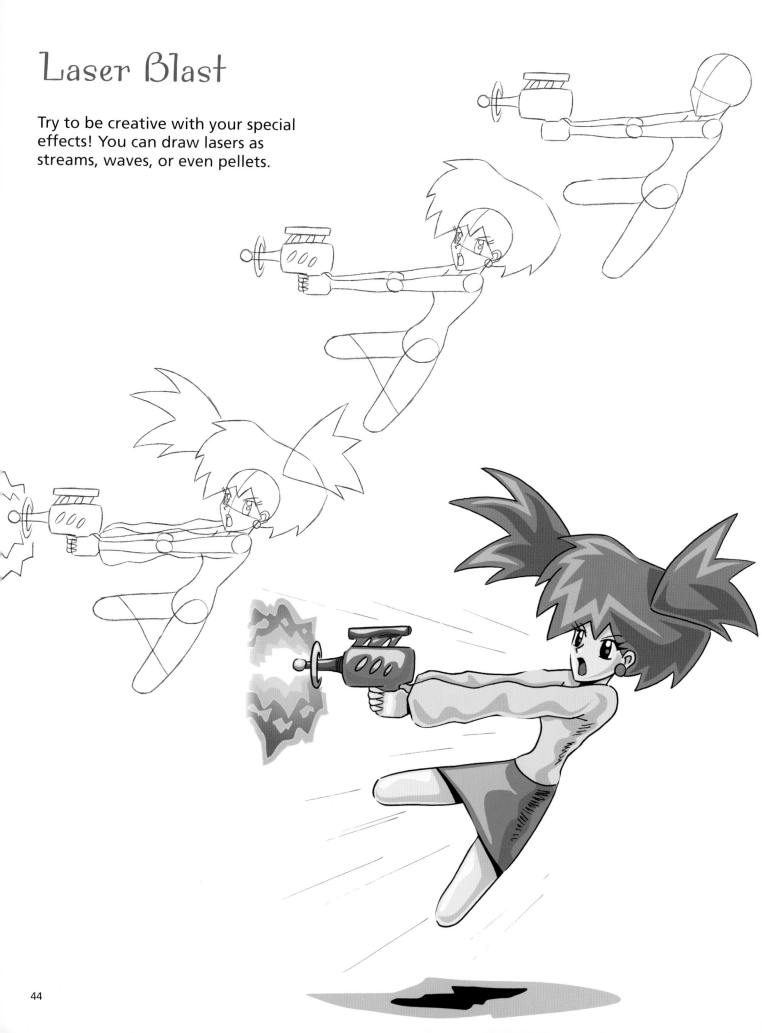

Leader of the Earth Rebels

A rebel leader has just gotta have a headset. That way he can bark orders while striking cool poses like this one. I like to put a little scratch mark, like a scar, on the faces of rebels and their leaders, to make them look scrappy.

Magic Sorceress

Evil characters always get to
wear the flashy clothes. Look
at how fancy her outfit is.
Villains are *never* modest!

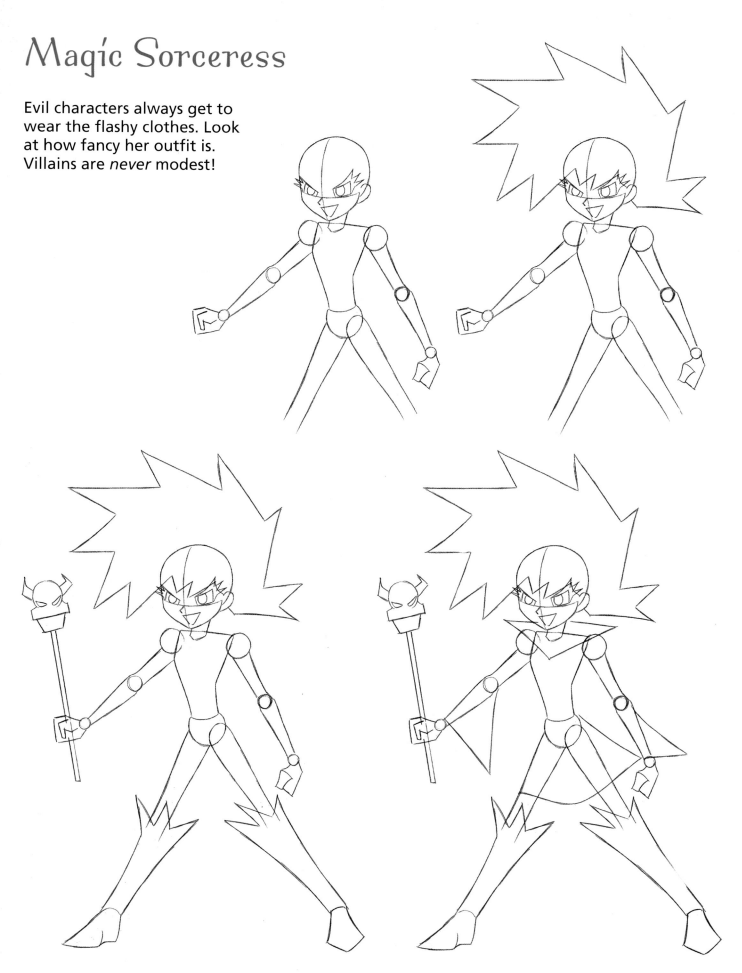

THE BATTLING ROBOTS OF JAPANESE COMICS!

Awesome giant robots are among the most popular and exciting characters in manga. You might think they look hard to draw, but they're not! If you can draw circles, ovals, rectangles, and squares, you can draw giant robots.

Mr. Colossus

Start with basic shapes and save the details for last. It's only in the last step that we get kind of fancy. Everything else is a matter of plopping one big shape on top of another.

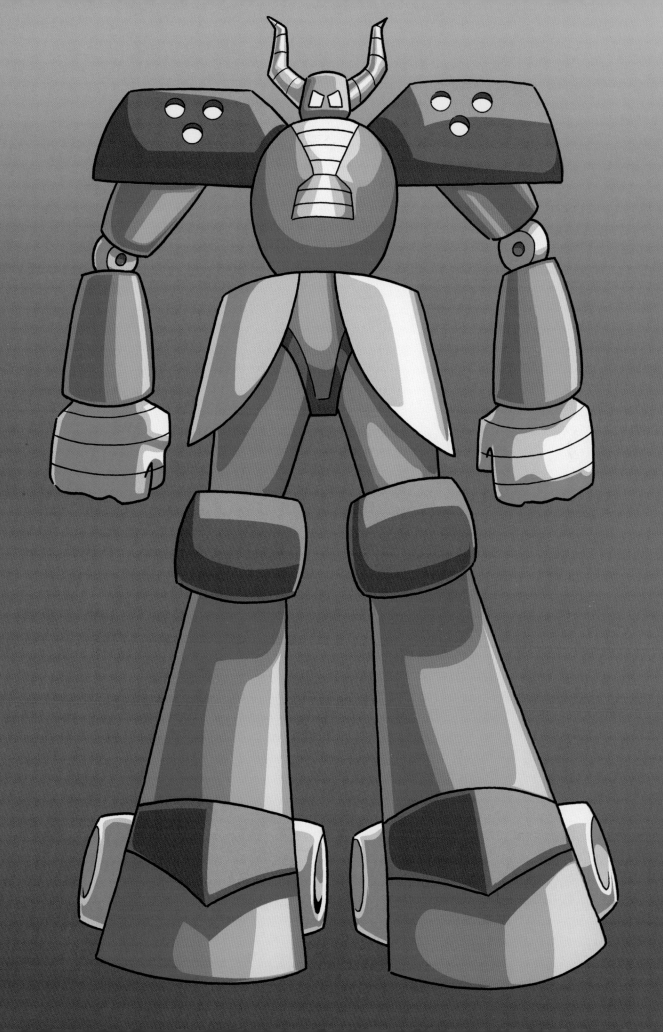

Using Arms as Weapons

Giant robots don't need to carry weapons—they *are* weapons! This powerful robot has forearms that are, in fact, laser rifles. Now, look at his eyes. Okay, so maybe he doesn't have eyes, but he has an eye guard. See how it makes a "V"? A "V" is the natural shape of a frown, and is often used for robot eyes. It makes the robot look intense. You want that in a giant robot.

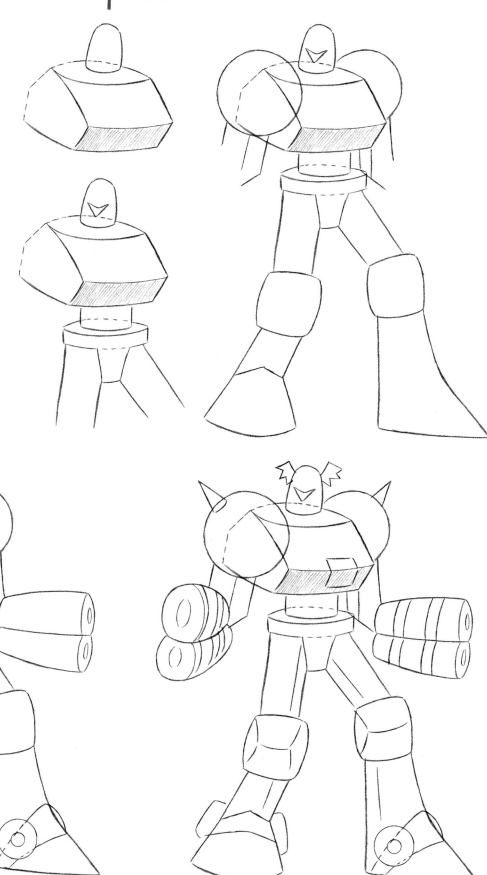

Flying Robot Soldier

The main part of this robot's body is an *octagon,* which is a shape with eight sides. Don't worry if each little section doesn't look exactly right—it's the overall effect we're after. Oh, and when you draw wings on a giant robot—any giant robot—make them huge. Little wings aren't impressive enough.

Laser Fighter

Doesn't this robot look intense? Want to know why? Simple: I gave him a big chest and made him really tall, but then gave him a tiny, mechanical-looking head. That makes him look like a fighting machine that is all strength without much smarts. Like a system programmed to destroy.

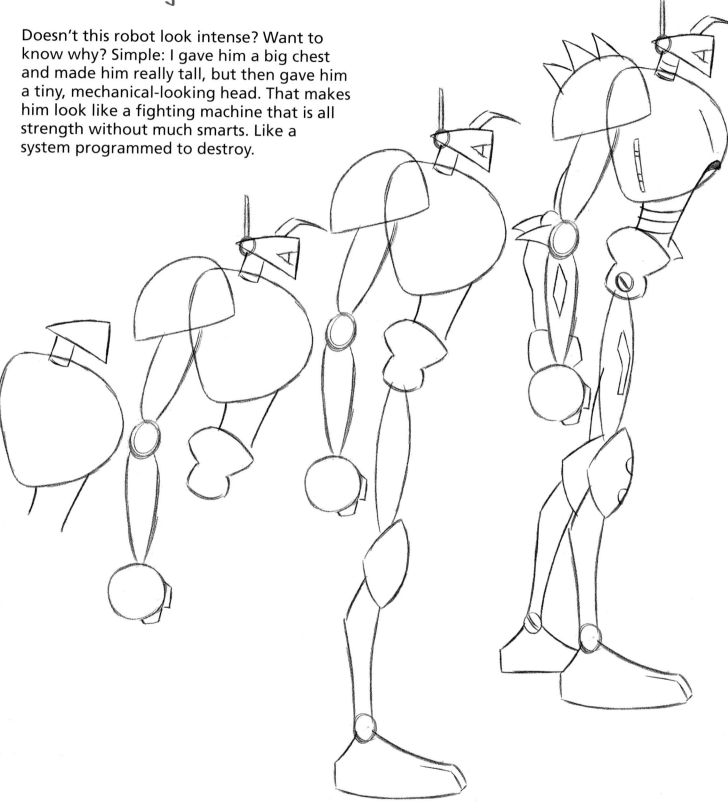

BONUS PAGES: ADVANCED DRAWINGS

Once you get the hang of drawing manga characters (and I know you will!), you may want to try something a little more challenging. These drawings may take a bit more practice, but they'll look great when you're done.

Extreme Perspective

In this drawing, everything looks like it's coming right at you. Here's the trick: Draw a big upper body, but tiny legs. And notice how the chest hides the stomach area completely—we don't even see it.

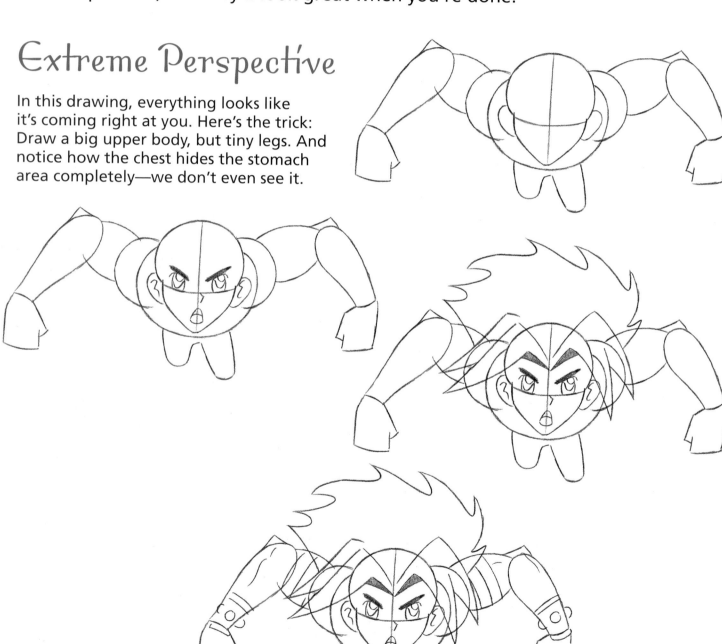

Stylish Teen

This may look like a tough pose to draw, but it's not. That's because the legs and arms are *symmetrical.* This means that both sides are the same. Both legs are in the same position, and both arms are in the same position.

Dark Magic

Manga is a fantasy world where you can let your imagination go wild. Notice how the speed lines make these creatures look like they've just jumped right out of the wizard's hands.

Spaceship Commander

When you design a character, try to come up with an outfit that shows the character's role in the story. What parts of this outfit make her look like a spaceship commander? She's got a jet pack, an insignia on her shoulders (the stars), gloves, kneepads, and—most typical of manga sci-fi characters— big, bulky, futuristic boots.

Play Ball!

Artists like to give their characters props to play with. An action as simple as throwing a ball can be turned into a futuristic scene by changing the ball into a mass of highly charged energy.

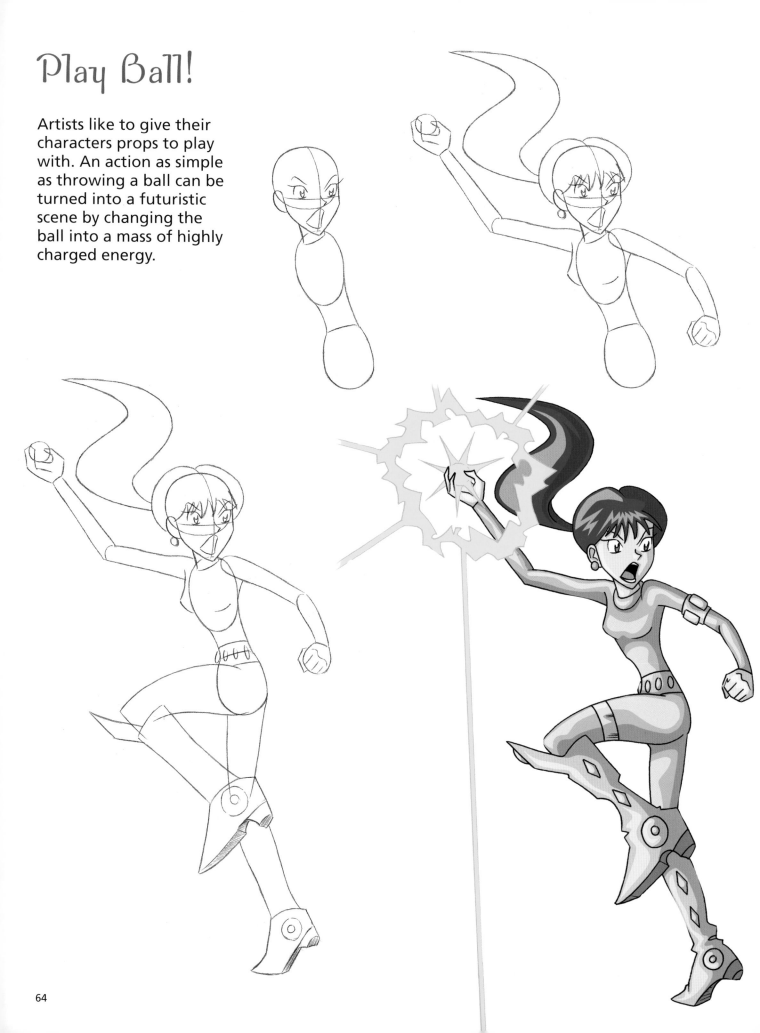

Monster Basics 70

BASIC HEAD CONSTRUCTION
SOME MONSTER HEAD SHAPES
CUTE, INNOCENT MONSTER EYES
MEAN, SNEAKY MONSTER EYES
DIFFERENT HEIGHTS FOR DIFFERENT CHARACTERS
FOUR LEGS OR TWO?
MANGA MONSTER HANDS

MANGA MONSTER FEET
JAW SIZE = BODY SIZE
CHUBBY IS BETTER!
ADDING THE RIGHT DETAILS
A BIT MORE ABOUT MARKINGS
SPECIAL POWERS
BE INVENTIVE AND MAKE MISTAKES!

Manga Monster Characters 84

SIMPLE-SHAPE CONSTRUCTIONS
CRABZILLA
TRIPLE-PIPPS
FIZZLE KITTY
ATOMIC BUNNY
CHIM-PU PET
BELCHOSAURUS
PLUMPINO
ZOT-ZOT 3
DINO-CRUSH
MOUSEPUFF
SPINTOP

UNIBEARS
CHIRPLE
TAILSTER
HOTHEAD SNEAKSTER
NEWMOO
BATTICA
PUDGE LORD
PURTAK
BOINGSTER
BABY-BOLTZ
WINGSTAR

MANGA BASICS

Most manga monsters are based on animals. Some look like common house pets; others look like wild animals; and still others look like dinosaurs. With only a few minor adjustments, you can turn an ordinary animal's face into a manga monster face! Isn't that surprising? Well, it's true, and it makes drawing manga monsters a whole lot easier. Just see for yourself!

Basic Head Construction

Let's start with a puppy's head, for example. The drawings in this book move step-by-step.

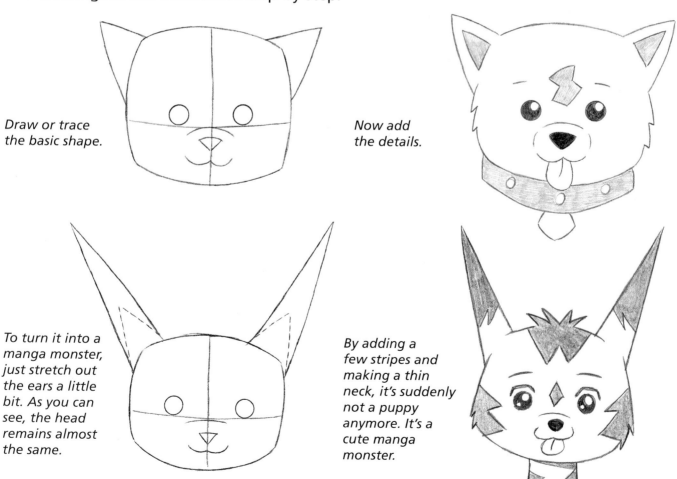

Draw or trace the basic shape.

Now add the details.

To turn it into a manga monster, just stretch out the ears a little bit. As you can see, the head remains almost the same.

By adding a few stripes and making a thin neck, it's suddenly not a puppy anymore. It's a cute manga monster.

Some Monster Head Shapes

Here are some of the most popular types of head shapes for you to work with. What do you notice about them? They're simple and round. Another thing to notice, which is *very* important, is that the eyes are placed low on the head. This is what gives the faces their turbo-charged cuteness.

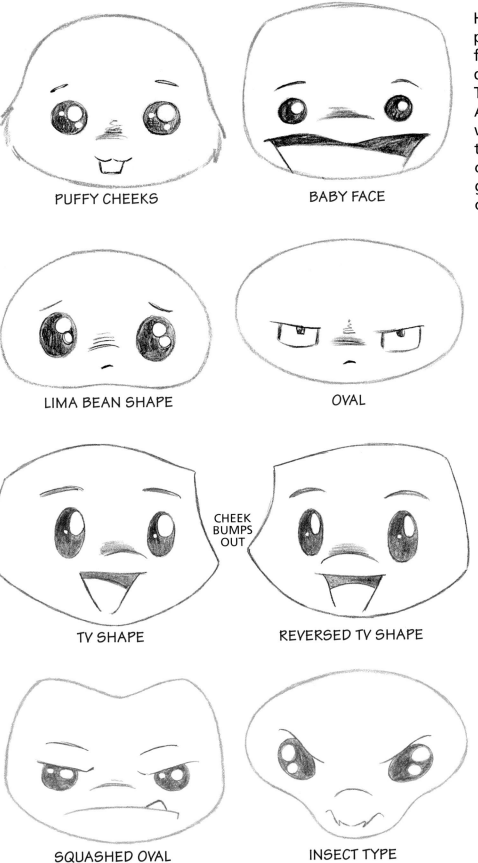

PUFFY CHEEKS

BABY FACE

LIMA BEAN SHAPE

OVAL

TV SHAPE

CHEEK BUMPS OUT

REVERSED TV SHAPE

SQUASHED OVAL

INSECT TYPE

Cute, Innocent Monster Eyes

Cute eyes are *always* large and round, with *big* eye-shines in them. Sometimes the eyes are drawn as only big pupils with shines inside. Other times, they are drawn as pupils floating inside the whites of the eyes. See what works for you. But either way, here's another very important hint: Make sure the eyes are spaced far apart. If you find that your character isn't looking cute enough, try spacing the eyes a little wider apart.

RECTANGLES

BUTTONS

BIG CIRCLES

TALL OVALS

EYE PLACEMENT

WRONG – NOT CUTE

RIGHT – CUTE

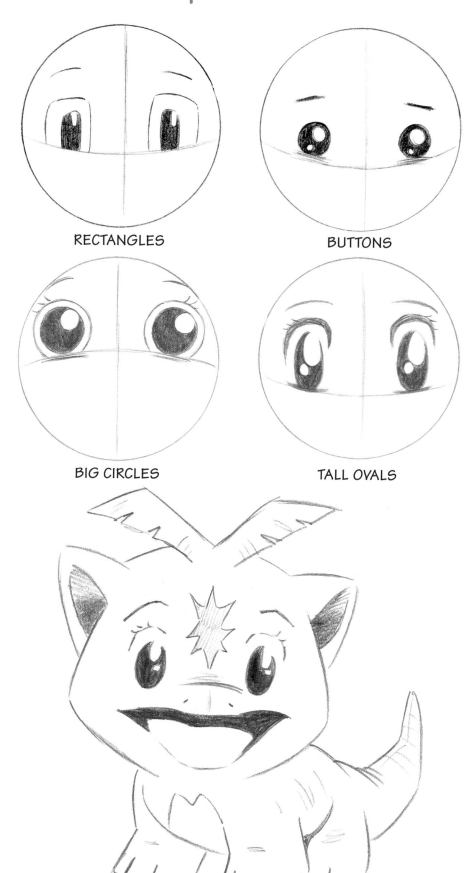

Mean, Sneaky Monster Eyes

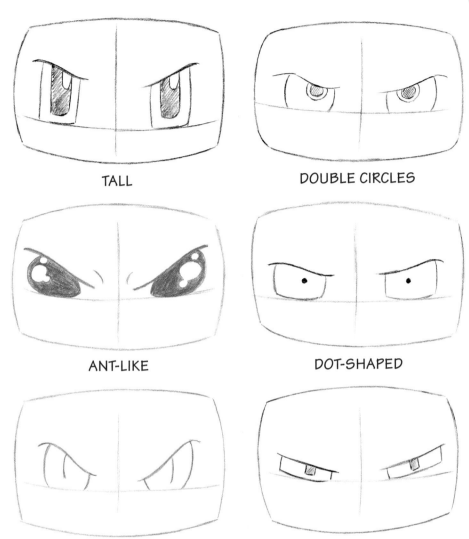

TALL

DOUBLE CIRCLES

ANT-LIKE

DOT-SHAPED

SNAKE-LIKE

SINISTER

Although cute eyes are fairly similar, there is a much wider variety of "tough" manga monster eyes from which to choose. Notice how different they are from the classic, innocent puppy eyes of the cute manga monsters on the previous page. Some are rectangular, some are tiny dots, while others are just slivers—like snakes' eyes. When drawing angry eyes, more often than not you should include the whites of the eyes, because it adds intensity.

Different Heights for Different Characters

It's a good idea to keep in mind the personality of the character when you're developing its height, because certain character types are best drawn tall, while others are better drawn short. For example, taller characters are usually weird and strange and not "cute" characters. Cute monsters are usually short, pudgy, and thick. Powerful characters are often drawn on all fours. However, these are only some helpful guidelines. Remember, always be creative, and make up your own rules if you want!

Smaller characters are usually cute.

Taller characters tend to be weird and strange.

Short, brawny characters that stand on all fours appear powerful and sturdy.

Many dinosaurs stood on all four legs.

ADD WEIRD EARS

ADD TEETH

By putting a dinosaur in an upright position, you can create a manga monster.

ADD ARM GUARDS

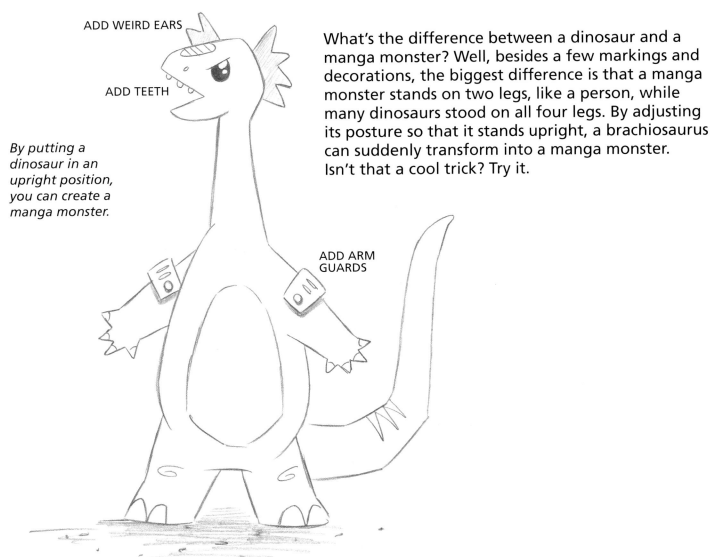

What's the difference between a dinosaur and a manga monster? Well, besides a few markings and decorations, the biggest difference is that a manga monster stands on two legs, like a person, while many dinosaurs stood on all four legs. By adjusting its posture so that it stands upright, a brachiosaurus can suddenly transform into a manga monster. Isn't that a cool trick? Try it.

Manga Monster Hands

You don't want to go to all the trouble of inventing a great manga monster character and then just stick ordinary hands on it. Hands are a part of the character design as well, so make sure you incorporate the monster's unique characteristics into all the body parts. Here are some examples.

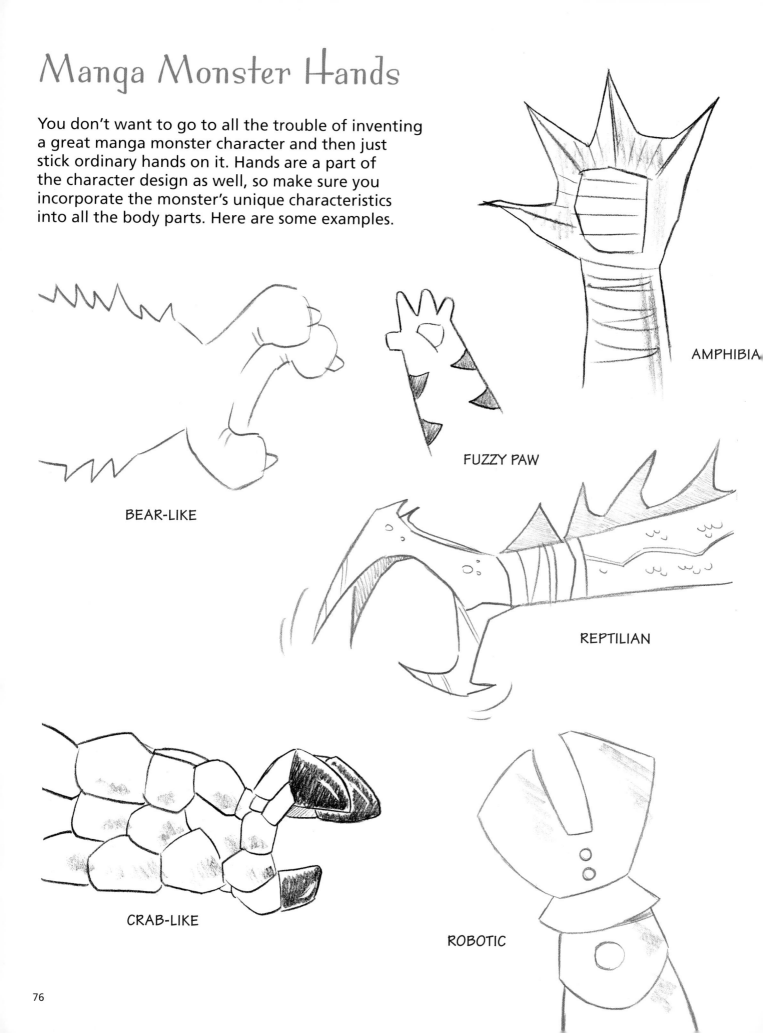

AMPHIBIA

FUZZY PAW

BEAR-LIKE

REPTILIAN

CRAB-LIKE

ROBOTIC

Manga Monster Feet

CAT-LIKE

Just like you chose your character's hands based on its traits, you will need to think about what its feet will look like. Are they huge, like an elephant's? Are they similar to a reptile's? Or maybe they look like a kitten's paw or an insect's skinny feet? Whatever you choose, be sure you have a definite idea in your head. Don't think to yourself, "They're only feet, so I won't bother to try to make them look good." If you spend an extra minute working on them, your character will look *extra* polished!

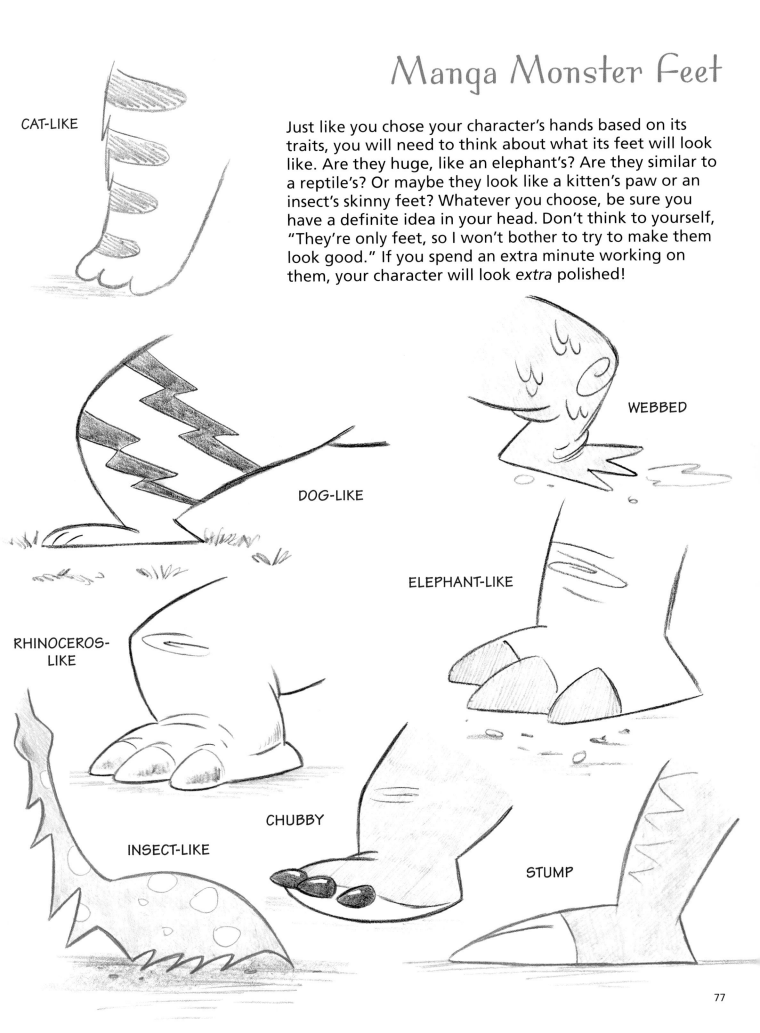

WEBBED

DOG-LIKE

ELEPHANT-LIKE

RHINOCEROS-LIKE

CHUBBY

INSECT-LIKE

STUMP

Jaw Size = Body Size

Here's a rule: The thicker the jaw is, the thicker the body has to be. So, if you're going to draw a character that looks as if it could chew through metal, then you have to make its body big. The opposite is also true: If you're drawing a character with a skinny face, then you can't give it a powerful-looking body. Look at the following examples and see if you agree.

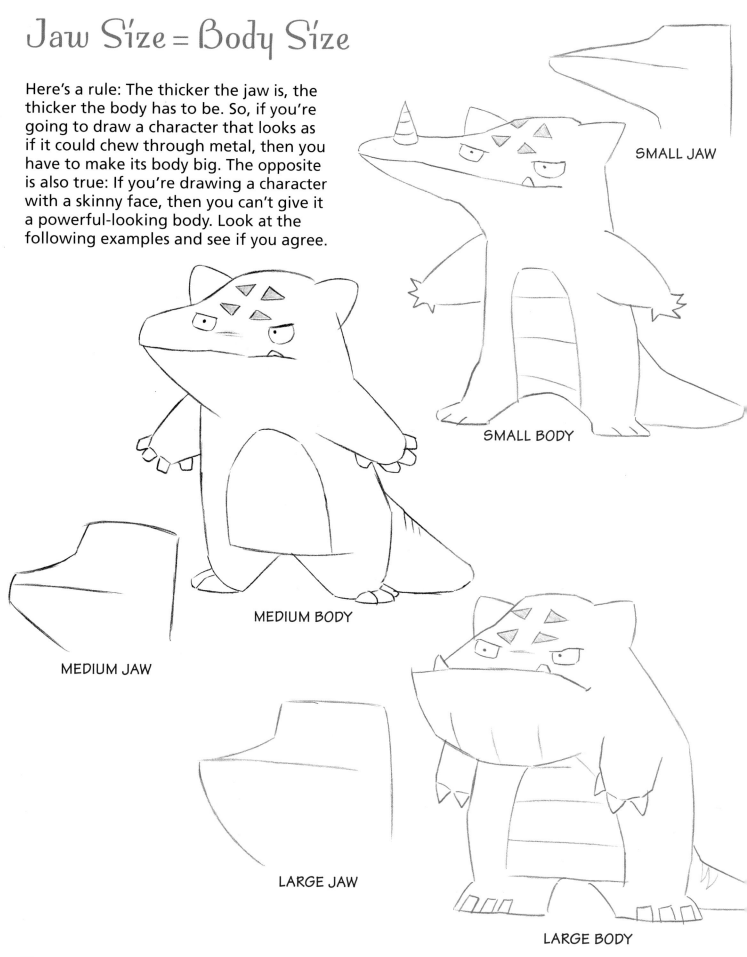

SMALL JAW

SMALL BODY

MEDIUM BODY

MEDIUM JAW

LARGE JAW

LARGE BODY

If you want to draw a manga monster that is appealing to all manga lovers, then pork him out! That doesn't mean he's got to be on a strict fries-and-soda diet, but he should be plump enough to squeeze, like an oversized stuffed animal you win at a carnival game. Skinny monsters look too much like reptiles!

CHUBBY
He's cute and squeezable! Who wouldn't love to have him for a friend or a pet?

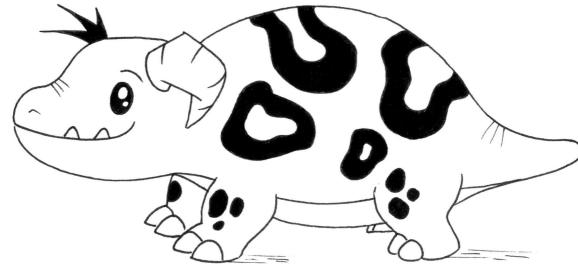

SKINNY
After three months on a low-carb diet, he looks like a reptile that would snatch flies with its tongue for lunch. Y-u-u-c-c-k-k-k!

HINT
A chubby monster also has chubby legs. If you decide to draw a skinny monster, you will have to draw leg joints, which you do not have to show on chubby types.

LEG JOINT

Adding the Right Details

As you just learned, manga monsters start out as pretty simple constructions. We then add a variety of details to the simple constructions to make them more fun and monstrous. By itself, each detail, or element, is not all that impressive, but when added together, they turn into a cool drawing!

We'll start with a basic construction in the first step. Then we'll add the extra details in the second and third steps to turn this manga character into a full-fledged monster—not a scary one, though. When this one says, "Boo!" you and your friends will have a tough time not giggling!

Make the head as big as the body.

SUPER FLARED EARS

Add the ears.

MOP-TOP HAIR

Short arms keep a character young-looking.

ANGLED HORNS

FOREHEAD MARKING

A Bit More About Markings

It's fun to decorate your manga monster, because, as you can see, it gives distinguishing features to your character. Without the markings, monsters would look too plain. Here are several views of the same monster to show you the classic places where markings are drawn.

TOP VIEW
A large splash marking is on the back.

BOTTOM VIEW
The large, ribbed underbelly travels from the tip of the chin, down the throat, all the way down the belly, partially into the legs, and to the tip of the tail.

SIDE VIEW
Half of one marking on the back can be seen in the side view, as well as some of the underbelly marking.

Special Powers

Now that we have the basic construction, body parts, details, and markings, we can give our characters special powers. Below, we have taken a triceratops and turned it into a manga monster with special powers that can come out of its tail.

You can easily come up with hundreds of special powers. The energy beams could come from the horns on its forehead, or the horns could shoot out of its forehead at his enemies, like projectiles, and be instantly refilled by more horns. Perhaps the monster's eyes could glow red, and beams could shoot out of them. Maybe the monster could even emit a force field around itself. If you can think it, it can happen!

Be Inventive and Make Mistakes!

Always remember, you don't have to stick to anything realistic. When you have a pencil in your hand, you're in charge! Let your imagination run wild. If you think of something funny or ridiculous, why not try it? What's the worst that can happen? If you don't like it, do what I do: Crumple it up, toss it in a recycling bin, and start over. That's the cool thing about drawing—mistakes don't count! A lot of beginners think that they have to get it right on the first try. As a professional cartoonist, I'm here to tell you that's not so. In fact, if you don't allow yourself to make mistakes, then you're not really expressing yourself enough.

There are a lot of good ideas buried deep inside your imagination. It's just that all of us artists have to dig through a bunch of mistakes before we get to the jewels. So dig deep, and don't be a perfectionist!

MANGA MONSTER CHARACTERS

Okay, I've given you a lot of secret techniques about how to draw manga monsters. Now we're going to move on to a really fun part of the book, where you get to take all of those art hints I gave you and use them to create all kinds of manga monster characters with different shapes, sizes, personalities, and powers!

This is going to be a step-by-step process. I suggest you draw the steps lightly at first. That way, you can erase if you make a mistake, and it's no big deal. When you finish the final step, draw over the lines that you like in bold pencil. Then erase the lighter "construction" lines and sketch marks that lead up to the final step. Or, you can simply trace over the final drawing to get a clean, finished image.

We'll first start with some monsters that are based on very simple shapes, like a circle, oval, and star. Simple shapes free you up, so you can focus all of your attention on the details, markings, and expressions. Now let's get started!

Simple-Shape Constructions

Here are several creatures that are built on very simple constructions. Still, we can find ways of turning them into convincing monsters. One way to spruce up a simple shape is to add lots of special effects and cool markings.

REPEATING FORMS
One way to turn an ordinary shape into an interesting monster is to repeat it. This insect-like creature is really just a bunch of circles stuck together.

CIRCLE
She's a floating puffball
with a ponytail.

CIRCLE WITH "EXTRAS"
This wacky vegetable monster is the
meanest, most vicious piece of salad this
side of the universe. Whatever you do,
don't let him catch you with a bottle
of ranch dressing in your hand!

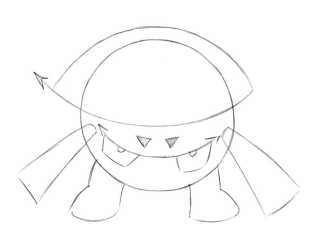

MULTIPLE CIRCLES

You can also use simple shapes within large simple shapes to create part of a character, such as the round head within the oval-shaped body. The rest of the body is then made up of large shapes. Poor little Pigcycle. He got a flat tire riding on his unicycle. Now he'll have to walk all the way home from the ice cream truck in his driveway to his front door. Sometimes life just isn't fair!

STAR

Even this guy starts out as a simple ball. Then we add the "points," and he becomes an evil starfish.

MADE-UP SHAPES
You can even make up your own simple shapes to use as a starting point for a character.

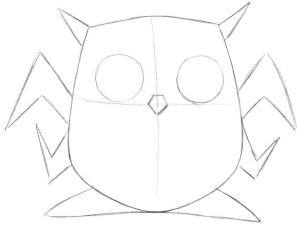

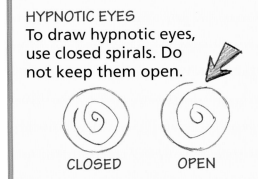

HYPNOTIC EYES
To draw hypnotic eyes, use closed spirals. Do not keep them open.

CLOSED   OPEN

SLITHERING FRIGHT
Without any markings or extra items added to this creature, it wouldn't be very interesting. But by adding a few—not too many—horns and other monster details, we can turn an ordinary garden snake into a fearsome manga monster.

Crabzilla

Now let's add a couple more steps to our basic shapes. This creature is a perfect example of a how a character that is easy to draw can still be chock-full of personality. The entire shape is really just built on a half circle. Of course, we have to chip away at it and add a few more things, but that's the fun part! You don't have to use the same colors I chose in the final monsters. Be creative and pick the colors that you like best!

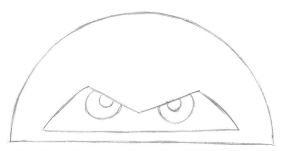

The "mask" around the eyes should widen out at the bottom.

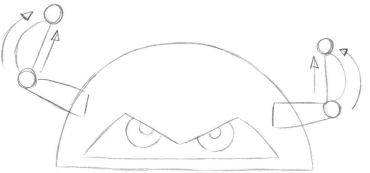

The forearm is made up of a curved line and a straight line. This gives the form variety. These types of concepts are called "graphic designs," and they are also applied to drawing cartoons.

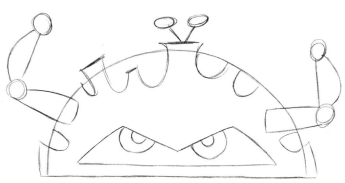

Extend parts of the shell past the outline and make indentations in the shell.

Giant claws are funny on such a small character. It makes it seem like he thinks he's so frightening, but we can't help but think he's just plain silly!

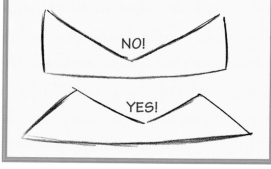

EYES
Look at the two eye structures below. The top one is straight at the ends, and looks like a pair of goggles. The bottom one widens at the ends, and gives a crab-like impression.

NO!

YES!

By blackening in the eye mask, you add a nice bit of contrast to the drawing and make the crab seem even more grumpy. Add some loopy radar lines around his antennae and some lightning bolts off his claws, and you've got a manga monster who can rule the world—or, at least, his section of the algae bed.

Triple-Pipps

If these guys were any cuter, I think I'd cry. They're so sweet that I could dunk them in my cereal every morning. This is another good example of the fun you can have when you start out with a very simple foundation, add a few elements here and there, and turn these nondescript characters into fun little guys with charm.

When drawing a group of characters, I always find it easier to complete a rough sketch of the main character first. It acts like an anchor for the rest of the composition.

The outer two characters lean to the left and to the right so that we can clearly see their faces.

Draw tall headpieces on each character. These headpieces will be their superpowers, conducting fields of electricity.

Look at all the added stuff we gave these simple characters to create full-fledged personalities.

SUPERCONDUCTIVE
ELECTRICAL HATS
AND ELECTRIC BOLTS

FOREHEAD MARKINGS

EAR HORNS

TECHNO-BELTS

Fizzle Kitty

Now that we've practiced some simple manga monsters, let's move on to some characters that are a little more challenging, like this little kitty with such big worries! His head takes up half the length of his entire body! Only cute characters have such exaggerated proportions.

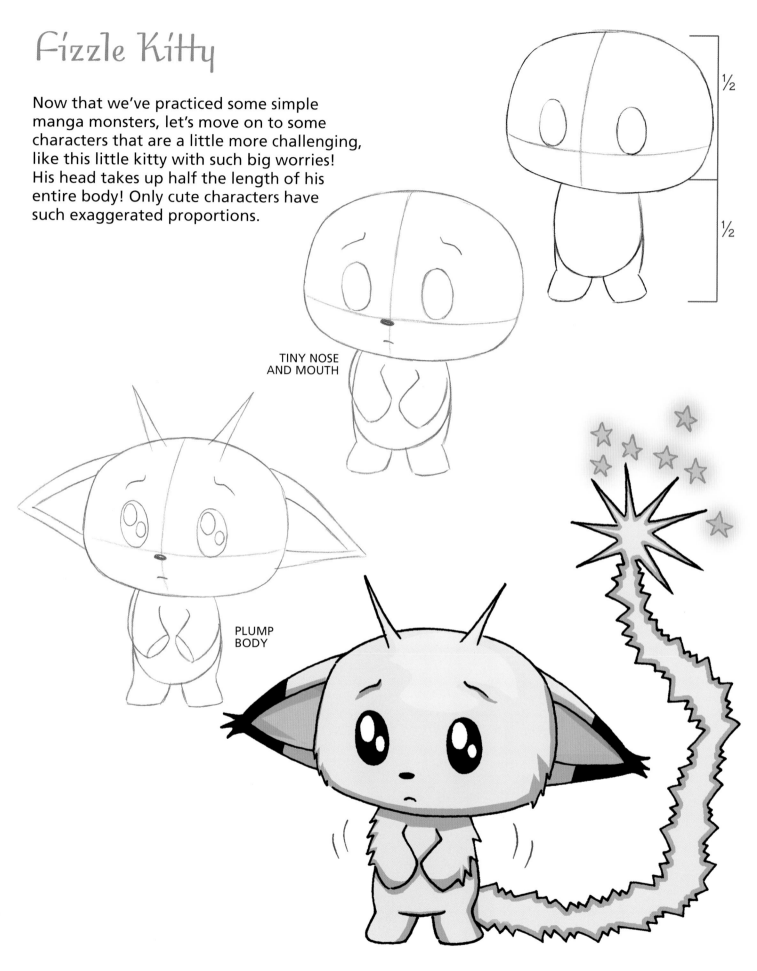

½

½

TINY NOSE AND MOUTH

PLUMP BODY

Atomic Bunny

You don't even have to give this character a nose, but a few whiskers help. Add subtle markings to the ears and arms, because you need to remind your viewer that this isn't a cute little rabbit.

MOP-TOP

NO NECK

SQUAT, LITTLE BODY

Draw both feet on the same level.

Create openings in the arms for atomic blasts.

Blasts widen as they explode.

Chim-Pu Pet

He's pampered and rich. And when not walking around his penthouse, he's being carried around in his owner's expensive designer handbag. Since this is a dainty little fella, make sure you draw him a bit toned-down and not too cartoonish. Big, round heads, little bodies, and small snouts are great combinations when trying to draw cute characters.

ROUNDED LIMBS

BIG EYE-SHINE

DELICATE MOUTH

TAPERED LEGS

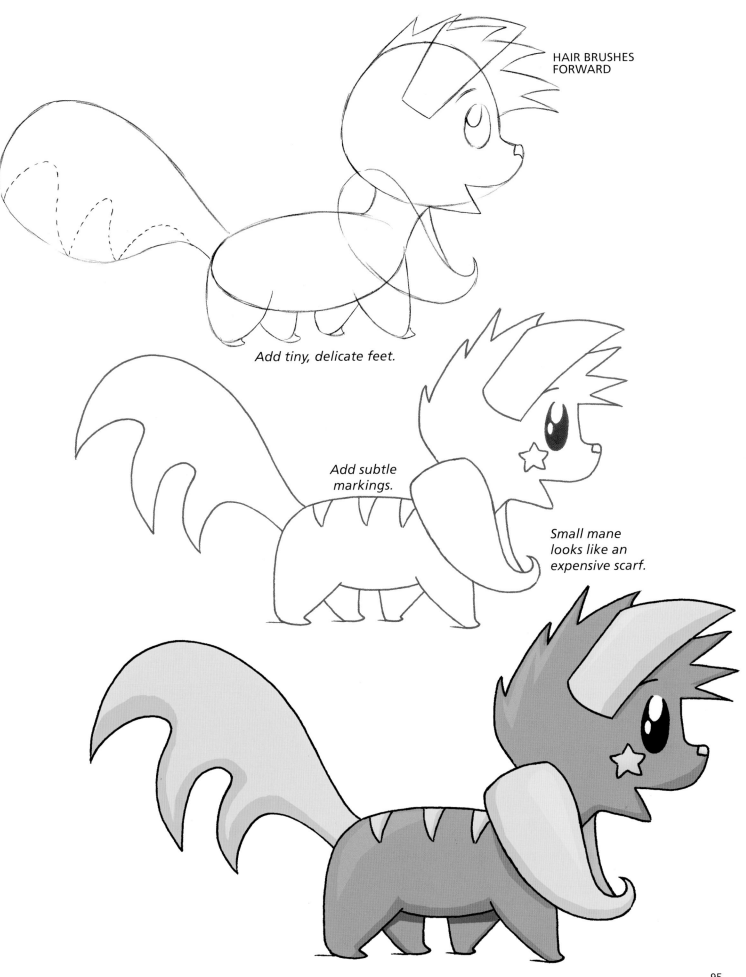

HAIR BRUSHES FORWARD

Add tiny, delicate feet.

Add subtle markings.

Small mane looks like an expensive scarf.

Belchosaurus

His belches are so loud that they actually shake the trees in the forest. Any time the other animals want some coconuts, they give Belchosaurus something to eat. He then lets out an earth-shattering *BELLLCCCH*, the trees shake, and the coconuts come tumbling to the ground! An extra-wide head means the character is nice, but dumb. Also, when a character is really fat, you don't have to draw a neck. Just stick the head on a big upper body.

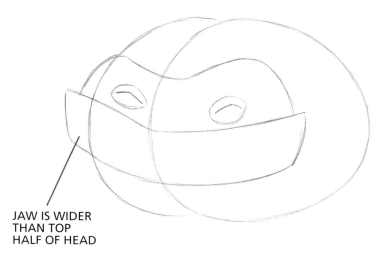

JAW IS WIDER THAN TOP HALF OF HEAD

FRONT HALF OF BODY OVERLAPS BACK HALF

ARMS ARE SPREAD WIDE TO SUPPORT MASSIVE WEIGHT

Plumpíno

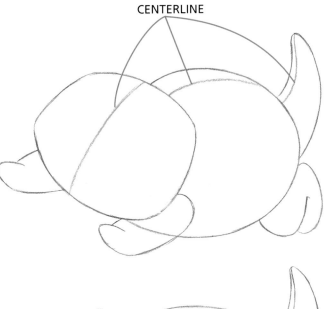

CENTERLINE

My favorite manga characters to draw are the roly-poly monsters that leap into the air to pounce after someone. To me, their attacks always look funny. I mean, how slow do you have to be to get caught? Like Belchosaurus on the previous page, this monster is fat, so apply the same techniques.

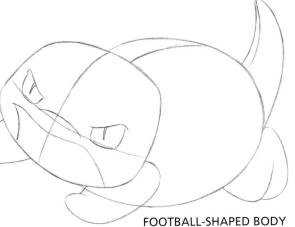

FOOTBALL-SHAPED BODY

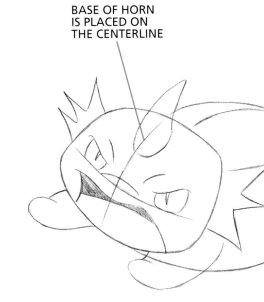

BASE OF HORN IS PLACED ON THE CENTERLINE

Zot-Zot 3

This character may be small, but she's a great friend when you're in trouble. Zot-Zot 3 will dash for help if you're ever in trouble! It doesn't matter if help is two blocks away, or fifty miles. She will keep running until she finds help!

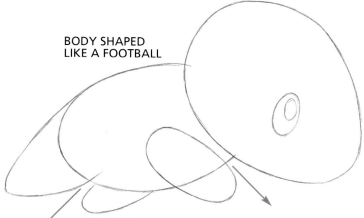

BODY SHAPED LIKE A FOOTBALL

ARMS AND LEGS STRETCH AWAY FROM EACH OTHER AT A 45° ANGLE TO SHOW EXTENSION

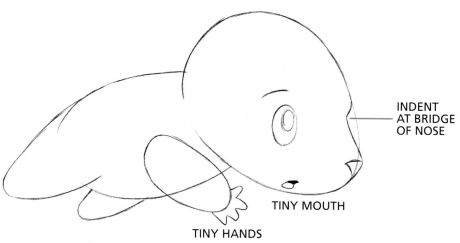

INDENT AT BRIDGE OF NOSE

TINY MOUTH

TINY HANDS

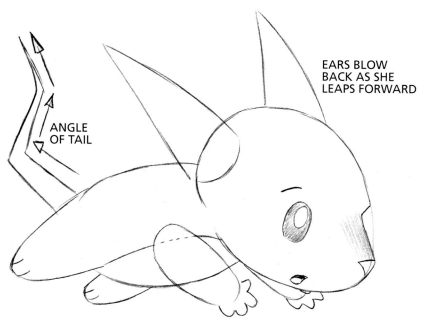

ANGLE OF TAIL

EARS BLOW BACK AS SHE LEAPS FORWARD

You must draw a shadow underneath a character when it is in the air. Otherwise, it will look like it is on the ground.

Dino-Crush

He's mean, tough, and extremely feared, and nobody—not even his own family—likes him. No, he's not a lawyer, but rather the manga-dinosaur monster, Dino-Crush. When he walks through the land, he destroys everything in sight. Hey, maybe he *is* a lawyer after all!

Just like the *Tyrannosaurus rex*, this guy has little arms. In the final drawing, add some warts and bumps to make him extra ugly—not that he was ever handsome to begin with! Also, add some extra details, like smoke or fire coming out of his nostrils.

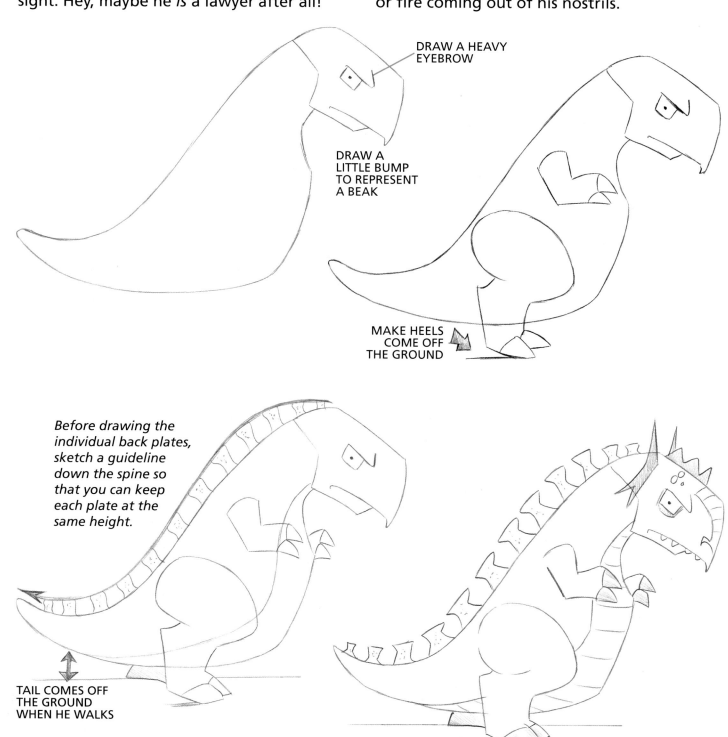

DRAW A HEAVY EYEBROW

DRAW A LITTLE BUMP TO REPRESENT A BEAK

MAKE HEELS COME OFF THE GROUND

Before drawing the individual back plates, sketch a guideline down the spine so that you can keep each plate at the same height.

TAIL COMES OFF THE GROUND WHEN HE WALKS

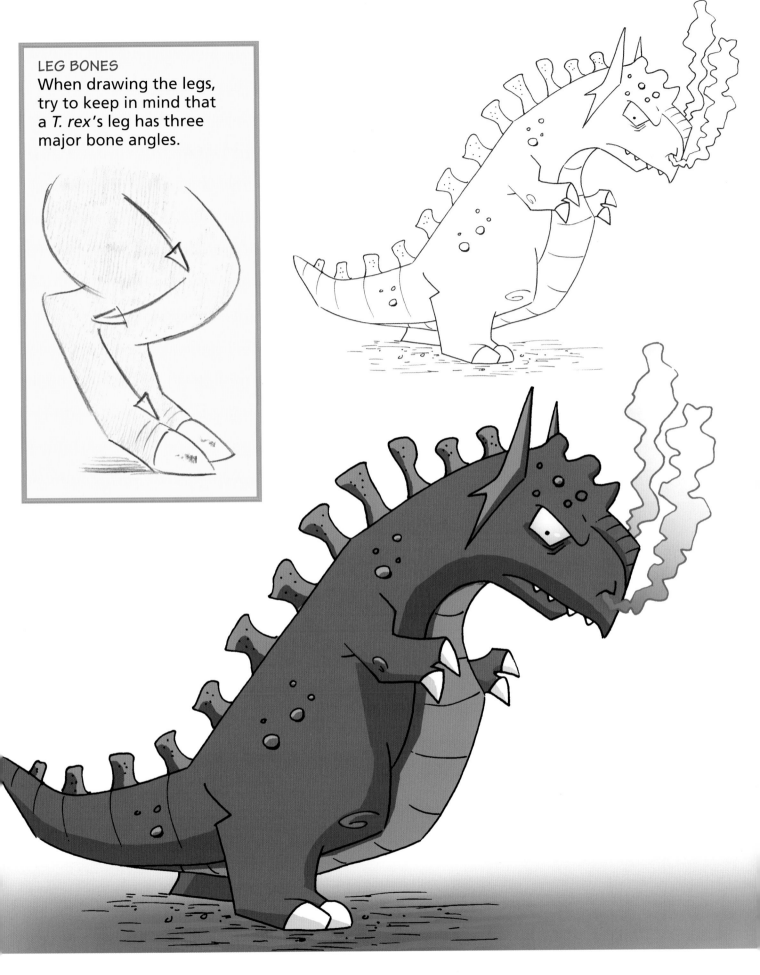

LEG BONES

When drawing the legs, try to keep in mind that a *T. rex*'s leg has three major bone angles.

Mousepuff

Run for your lives! Here comes Mousepuff! Just kidding. If there's anything more harmless than Mousepuff, I've never seen it. This little creature lets off a cute little *squeak* every time it's squeezed.

Draw a reversed TV-shaped head, like we talked about on page 71. Notice that the head is bigger than the body. Draw tall ovals for the eyes.

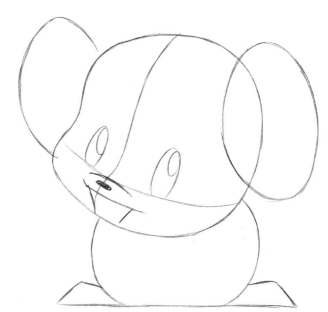

Draw two circles for the ears.

Draw a small and chubby arm.

Spintop

When a really cute manga monster character is called for, artists usually apply big ears and wide cheeks. Also, look at the eyes. They're perfectly round, which is common in many—but not all—manga monsters.

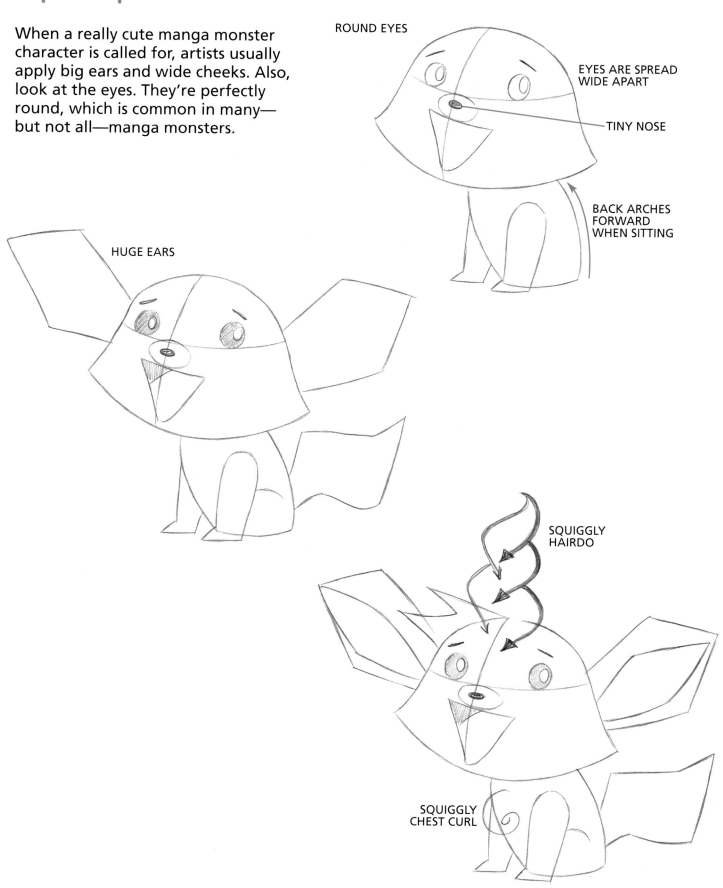

ROUND EYES

EYES ARE SPREAD WIDE APART

TINY NOSE

BACK ARCHES FORWARD WHEN SITTING

HUGE EARS

SQUIGGLY HAIRDO

SQUIGGLY CHEST CURL

Unibears

Shh! Don't speak too loudly. You might frighten the Unibears, the poor little things. They get upset so easily. Even the sound of blowing bubbles can make a Unibear cry!

Draw a wide oval. Then, push the middle up, which will be the chin, and then tug the ends down, which will be the cheeks.

Stack the Unibears in a row (they like to hide behind one another).

Chirple

Check out this mechanical canary from the future! What will science come up with next? I know, this character is a little more husky than a real canary, but remember our rule of thumb: Manga monsters are always cuter when they're plump! Notice that the wings do not have a lot of feathers. Just a few oversized curves do the trick.

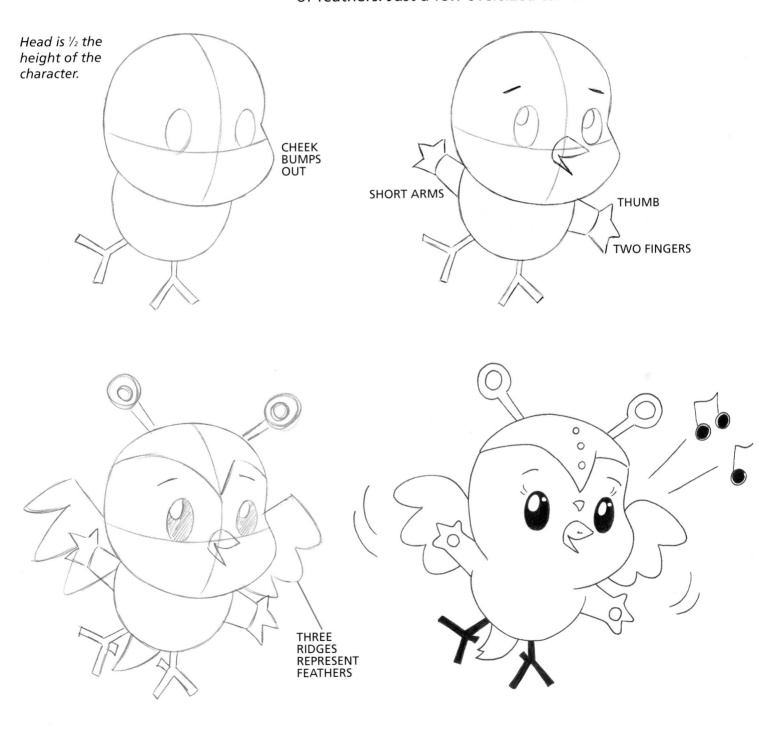

Head is ½ the height of the character.

CHEEK BUMPS OUT

SHORT ARMS

THUMB

TWO FINGERS

THREE RIDGES REPRESENT FEATHERS

Tailster

You can use body language to give even the tiniest characters big attitudes. With fists planted firmly at its sides, this angry mouse's posture tells us that it is fed up and is not going to play nice anymore!

Characters with almond-shaped eyes tend to look evil, not cute. Another thing you might notice is that it is missing the cuddly cheeks that cute manga monsters have, which also tells us that it means business!

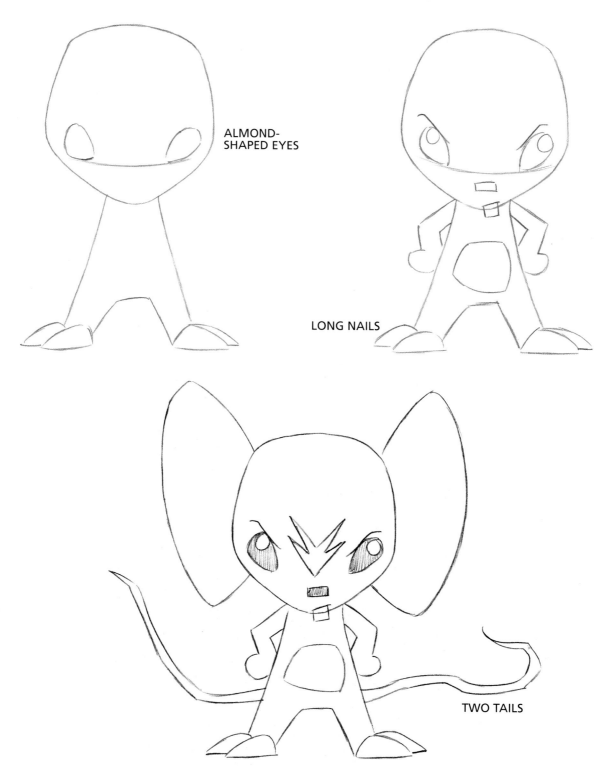

ALMOND-SHAPED EYES

LONG NAILS

TWO TAILS

Hothead

Take a look at this crazy character. Remember what I've been telling you about the eye placement in cute characters. Cute characters *always* have their eyes placed low on the head. Well, look at this guy. He's not cute, is he? And look where his eye is placed. It's high up on the head, isn't it? So you see,

where you place the eye really does make a difference in how the character is perceived.

Since this character is funny, and not really scary, we'll give it teeth, but we'll make sure they aren't really sharp. We'll also use two different tones on its markings on the back so that we can have fun with different colors.

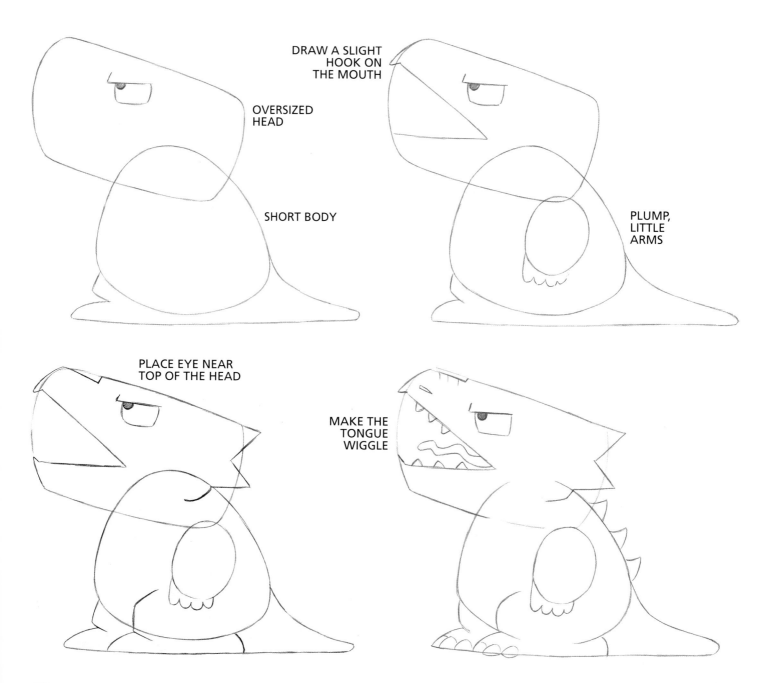

DRAW A SLIGHT HOOK ON THE MOUTH

OVERSIZED HEAD

SHORT BODY

PLUMP, LITTLE ARMS

PLACE EYE NEAR TOP OF THE HEAD

MAKE THE TONGUE WIGGLE

Sneakster

When you want a character to have a sneaky expression, give it half-closed eyes and a toothy grin. It's important that the eyes close from both the bottom *and* the top, because that's what makes a shifty smile. Would you trust anything this gigantic lizard tells you?

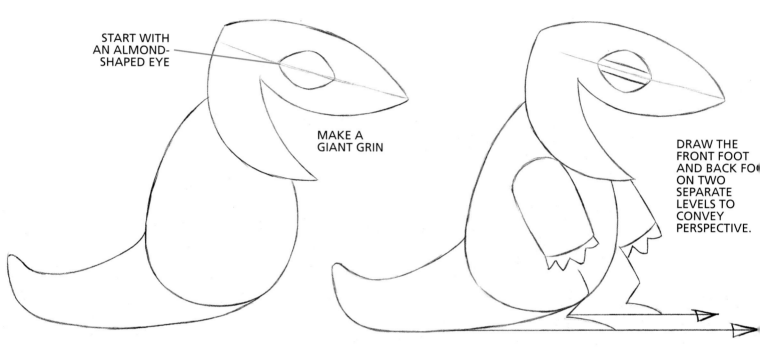

START WITH AN ALMOND-SHAPED EYE

MAKE A GIANT GRIN

DRAW THE FRONT FOOT AND BACK FOO ON TWO SEPARATE LEVELS TO CONVEY PERSPECTIVE.

A SNEAKY EYE
To give this character a sneaky look, begin with a diamond shape. Add two lines in the middle, which will be the top and bottom eyelids. Add the eyeball.

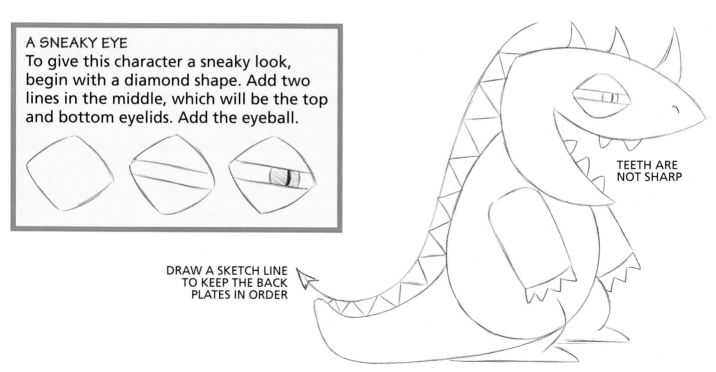

TEETH ARE NOT SHARP

DRAW A SKETCH LINE TO KEEP THE BACK PLATES IN ORDER

Newmoo

Face it, cows that stand up on two legs are just plain funny. With a silly udder and bad posture, it's a hoot. Also, I love grumpy cows. Draw a flat eyebrow to put it in a cranky mood. Then stand it up on two legs, add some cool markings, and you've got yourself a manga monster cow!

The markings on this cow are really fun. Little rectangles tossed randomly around the body give it a different look. Add spikes at the end of the horns to make it different from regular cows. Also add some spiked hair pieces that brush forward off its head.

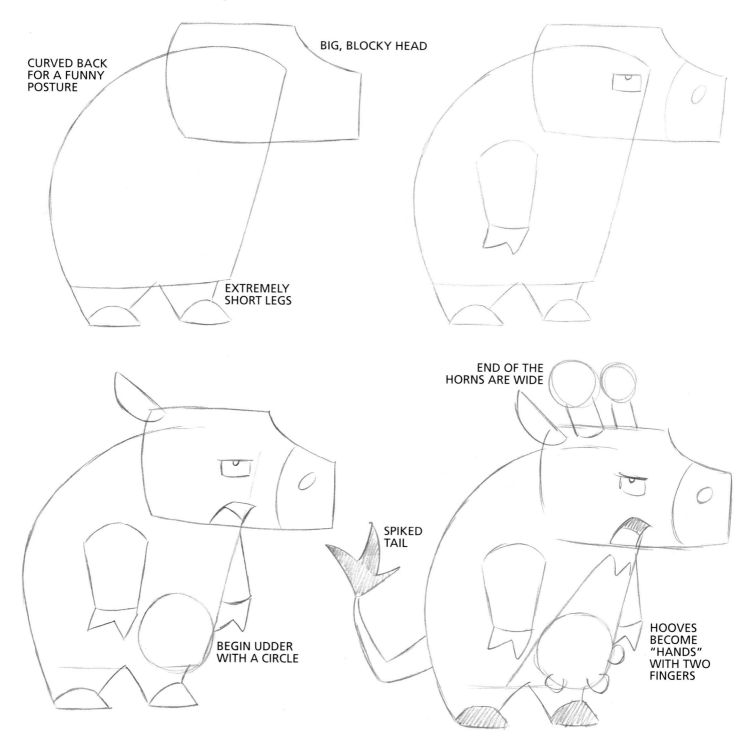

CURVED BACK FOR A FUNNY POSTURE

BIG, BLOCKY HEAD

EXTREMELY SHORT LEGS

END OF THE HORNS ARE WIDE

SPIKED TAIL

BEGIN UDDER WITH A CIRCLE

HOOVES BECOME "HANDS" WITH TWO FINGERS

Battica

This poor little vampire is afraid of the dark! Giant feet on a small body turn a regular character into a goofy one.

Another way to give your characters an authentic manga look is to make sure that the tongue takes up most of the space inside the mouth when it is wide open. Interestingly, American-style characters keep most of the space inside an open mouth empty.

GIANT FEET ALWAYS MEAN A GOOFY CHARACTER

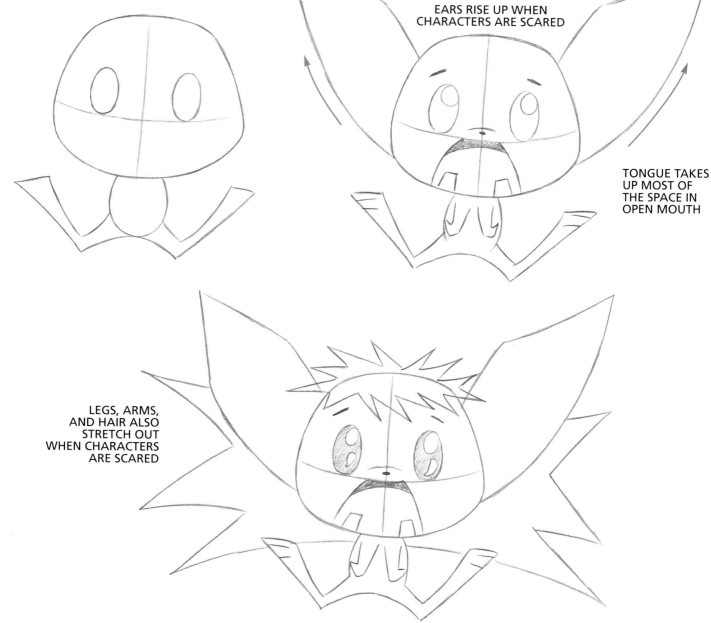

EARS RISE UP WHEN CHARACTERS ARE SCARED

TONGUE TAKES UP MOST OF THE SPACE IN OPEN MOUTH

LEGS, ARMS, AND HAIR ALSO STRETCH OUT WHEN CHARACTERS ARE SCARED

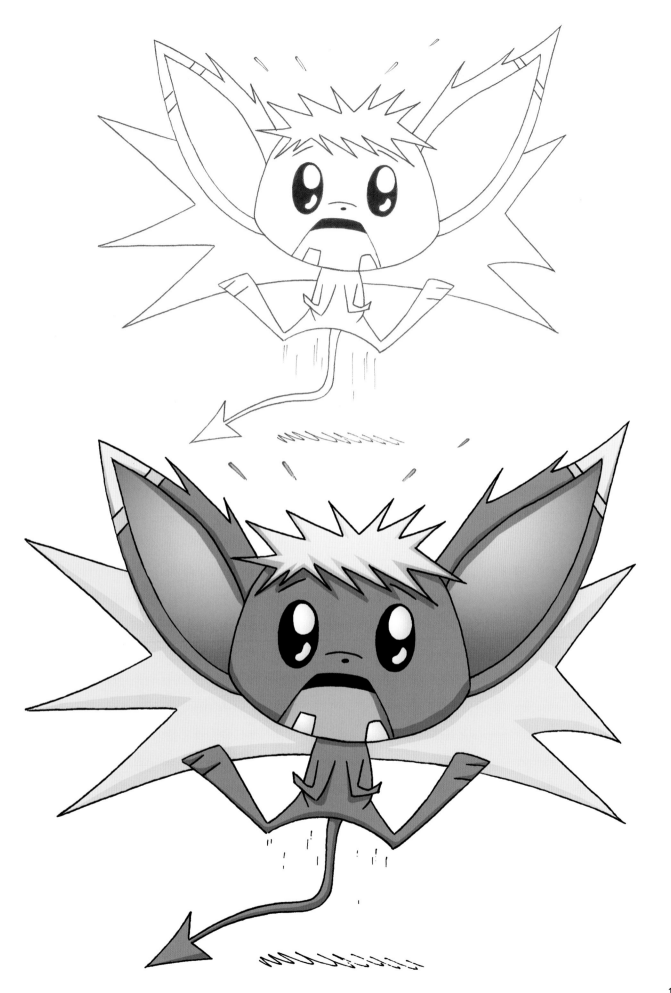

Pudge Lord

A martial arts expert who knows jujitsu, this character is the most feared monster at the buffet. You'll notice that he's in a ready stance: feet spread apart and arms at the sides. That means he's ready for anything that may come his way: monsters, evil fighters, winged creatures, jelly doughnuts, and even the dreaded tuna casserole! You can draw the mouth as a straight line, but I think it's more interesting to use a slightly curved line.

HEAD IS HORIZONTAL

BODY IS VERTICAL

When both eyes are on the same side of the face, the character becomes funny.

ARMS ARE REALLY SHORT

VERY TINY EARS

ANTENNAE

To make a character even funnier, draw both nostrils on the same side of the face.

THE UNDERSIDE
OF A HAND
When we *can* see
the underside of
a hand, draw the
edge of the hand
curving down.
When we *cannot*
see the underside of
the hand, draw the
edge of the hand
curving up.

119

Purtak

This little monster would make a good house pet. The only problem is that she gets very, very jealous. And if she senses you have been petting someone else's dog or cat, she will rip all of your clothes to shreds and have an accident on your homework. Other than that, she's as sweet as can be.

When drawing a manga monster standing on all fours and looking directly at you, shift the character slightly to one side to show one of its back legs. If you were to draw a manga monster on all fours facing straight forward, you wouldn't be able to see the back legs, which would make the character look flat.

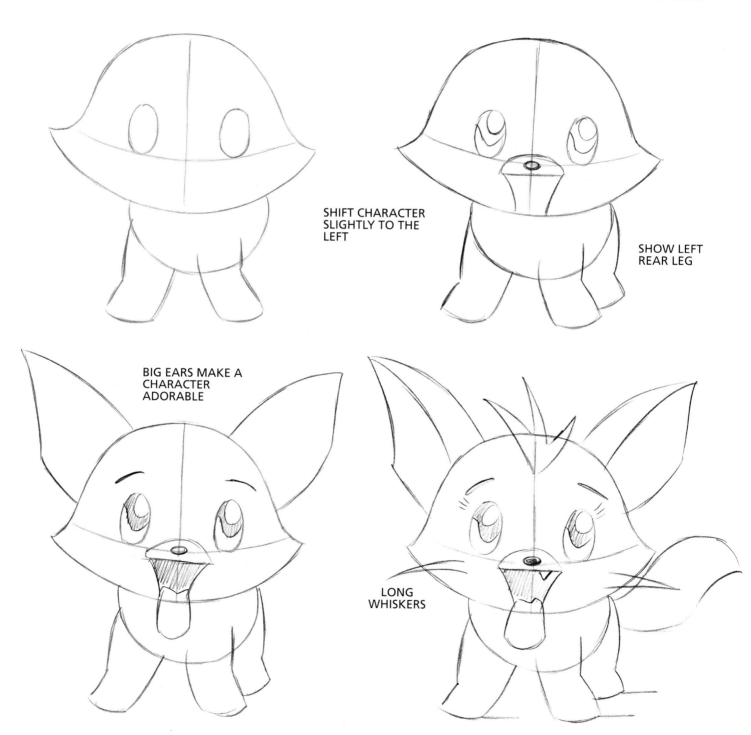

SHIFT CHARACTER SLIGHTLY TO THE LEFT

SHOW LEFT REAR LEG

BIG EARS MAKE A CHARACTER ADORABLE

LONG WHISKERS

THE MANGA LIP
The top lip of a manga character is flat when it is smiling. Compare it to an American character smile, in which there is a curve.

MANGA-STYLE   AMERICAN-STYLE

Boingster

Why walk around when you've got a spring attached to your bottom, and you can bounce? Makes sense to me. This character's face is easy to draw, because all of the features are gathered in the middle. The eyes are just two curved lines. The pose is also easy to draw, because the feet stick out toward us. Notice that the feet are just large ovals.

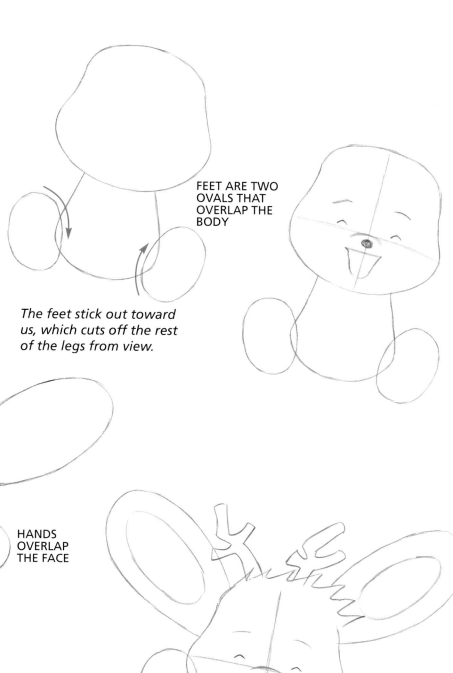

FEET ARE TWO OVALS THAT OVERLAP THE BODY

The feet stick out toward us, which cuts off the rest of the legs from view.

HANDS OVERLAP THE FACE

Draw the bottom of the legs as a single, curved line.

Give this critter a pair of antlers on its head and a coil on its backside. The ears shoot out at a 45° angle. Also, stretch out all of its limbs.

Baby-Boltz

Big powers come in small packages, and you do not want to mess around with this little squirt. She'll bring a storm of lightning down on anyone who messes with her bottle of milk! Even though she's a monster, we'll give her classic baby proportions.

BIG HEAD

CHUBBY CHEEKS

SMALL BODY

SHORT ARM

OVERSIZED BOTTLE (COMPARED TO SIZE OF THE FIGURE)

DOWNWARD EYEBROW TO SHOW CONCENTRATION

GIANT EYES

NO NOSE

SMALL, CHUNKY ARMS

FEET TURN INWARD, TOWARD EACH OTHER

CHUNKY LEGS

The beam of energy blasts from the center of her forehead. For a dynamic effect, make it jagged and draw different layers inside.

Drawing a "horizon line" makes the character look like she is sitting on the ground and not floating on the page.

Wingstar

Horses are often challenging for beginners, as well as intermediate artists, to draw. The main reason is that the joint configuration of the limbs is a little tricky. But, if we make our manga character a pony, then we can lose the hard angles of the limbs and make it not only easier to draw but much more appealing, too.

HINDQUARTERS

CHEST AREA

Draw a gently curved neck.

Ponies have shorter legs than horses.

The legs should be very straight.

MAKE A SMALL POINT AT THE SHOULDER

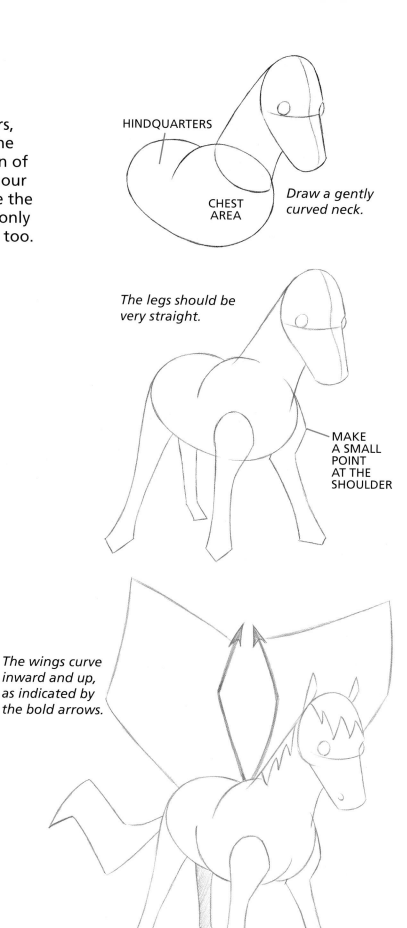

See how the hooves are created? Use two lines for each hoof, which peak in the middle, like a pyramid. The arrow shows you where to add a line to give definition to the chest and waistline.

EARS TILT FORWARD

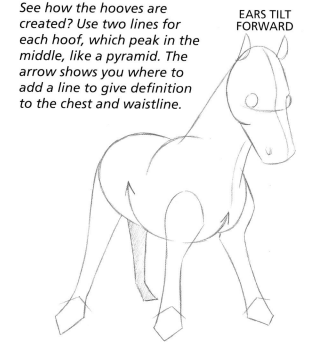

The wings curve inward and up, as indicated by the bold arrows.

Give your pony shiny black eyes for a sweet and innocent look—you know, the type of look you give your mom when you want something!

Shoujo Basics 130

DRAWING FACES
CREATING GIRL CHARACTERS
CREATING BOY CHARACTERS
DRAWING BISHIES
CREATING BISHIE CHARACTERS
DRAWING EYES

DRAWING THE FEMALE BODY
DRAWING THE MALE BODY
DRAWING THE BISHIE BODY
DRAWING SEATED CHARACTERS
DRAWING HANDS
DRAWING FEET AND SHOES

School Comics 152

UNIFORMS FOR GIRLS
UNIFORMS FOR BOYS
STUDENT ATHLETE
CHEERFUL TEEN
JOE COOL

TEEN IDOL
LUNCH BREAK
BACKPACK BOY
SIDEWALK RACER

Magic Time 164

MAGICAL GIRLS
MAGICAL GIRL WITH CAPE
FANTASY FIGHTER
HERO GIRL
MAGICAL BOY

PLANETARY COMMANDER
BOY WITH SPECIAL POWERS
GALLANT KNIGHT
DEMIGOD
GODDESS

Fairies and Friends 182

FAIRY GIRL
FANTASY PRINCESS

ELFIN QUEEN
FLYING FAIRY

SHOUJO BASICS

Ready to get started? Get your pencil and paper, and let's draw the basic shoujo-style head. Soon you'll be creating your own great shoujo characters!

Drawing Faces

Here's a typical, cheerful shoujo girl in a front view. See the crisscrossed lines on the first drawing? These guidelines will help you place the features on the face. The guidelines also let you make the eyes even with each other.

FRONT VIEW

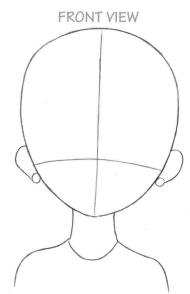

Draw light lines to guide you, then erase them at the end.

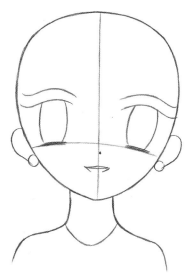

The nose starts as just a tiny dot. The top and bottom of the eyes are cut off by the eyelids.

Start penciling in details at this stage. Thick eyebrows and long bangs add to the shoujo look.

Details on the eyes add sparkle!

SIDE VIEW

Now we'll draw a boy in a side view, which is also called a "profile." The key to getting a good profile is drawing the nose in a sweeping curve. Shoujo boys also have receding chins—that is, they slope in rather than jutting out. Like girls' eyes, boys' eyes take up a lot of room on the face. The upper line of the eye is dark, and the bottom line is not. Look how the hair and eyes show this boy's personality!

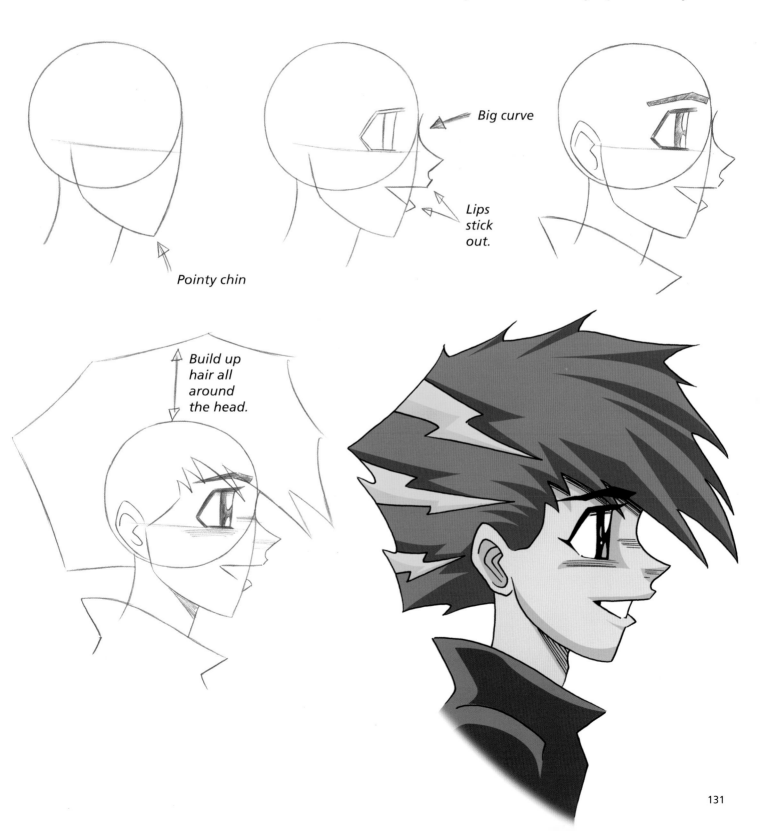

Big curve

Lips stick out.

Pointy chin

Build up hair all around the head.

THREE-QUARTER VIEW

The three-quarter view is halfway between the front and side views. It's a popular pose, and it's my favorite, because it makes characters seem more lifelike. To make it simple, I've broken the process down into easy-to-follow steps, so that you can draw along with me.

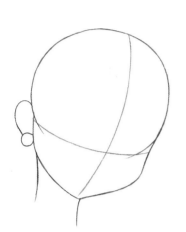

The center guideline is curved in this pose, never straight.

Perky smile!

Bangs usually go right down to the eyes.

Flowers in the hair add a nice touch.

Thick eyelids

Hair falls in front of ears, a classic look in shoujo.

You can see the eyebrows through the hair.

Now let's look at a boy in a similar pose.

Guideline for the eyes

When you're sketching the basic shape of the head, don't press too hard. You'll want to erase the extra lines when you're finished and don't want them too dark. If you do press hard, just trace your drawing on a new sheet of paper, keeping only the lines you want.

Sometimes I leave the line of the bottom lip unfinished, which gives the smile a gleaming look.

Shoujo boys look young and friendly.

Creating Girl Characters

Most female shoujo have certain traits in common. Use this page as a checklist when drawing your own characters. Bows, hair in a bun, flowers, or tiaras are frequently used to add a touch of femininity. Note the strands of hair that fall in front of the ears—they are typical in shoujo.

Big hairstyle

Eyebrows arch high above the eyes.

Thick lashes

Big eye shines

Soft curve to the face

Delicate nose

Small lips

Creating Boy Characters

Shoujo boys have an open, eager look. How do you show that personality in a drawing? Give your boy characters square jawlines and bright eyes. This boy is a good example: His eyebrows are thick and straight without eyelashes. Wild hair, styled or maybe a little messy, looks great!

Wild hair, often spiked

Thick eyebrows

Hair flops in front of eyes.

Eyes are more square than a girl's eyes.

Lines (called "sketch marks") on cheeks and nose

Sturdy neck

Adam's apple

Drawing Bishies

FRONT VIEW

The leading men of shoujo are dashing characters! In Japan, they are called Bishies, short for *bishonen,* which means "handsome man." While boys and girls have rounded faces, Bishies have long, thin faces. Their features are delicate: narrow eyes, sharp eyebrows placed right on top of the eyes, and long noses. Often, they have long hair parted down the middle.

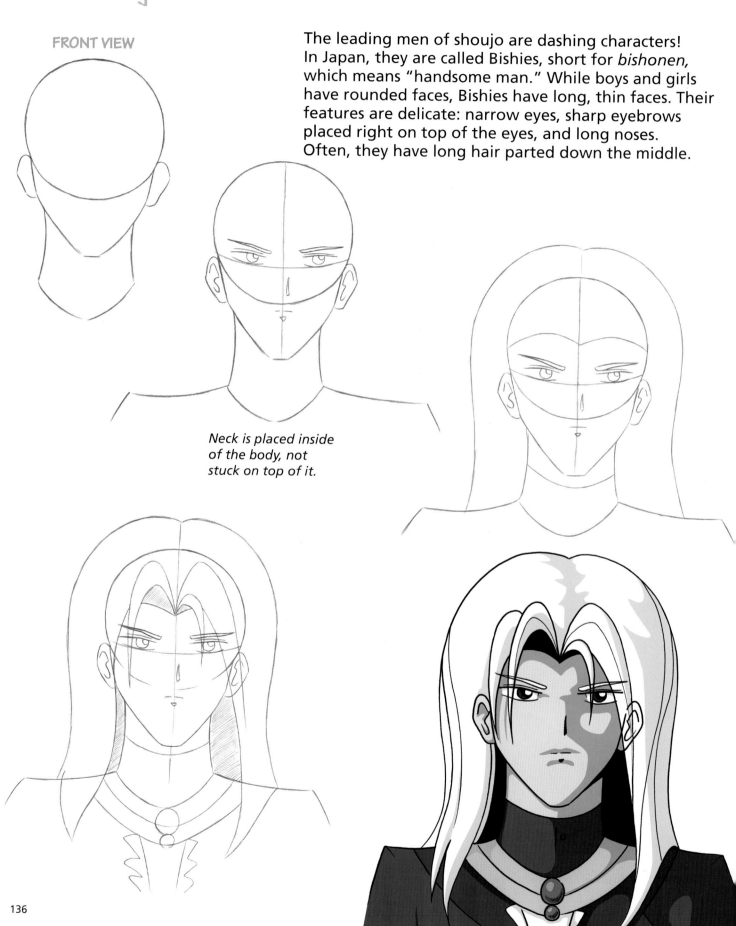

Neck is placed inside of the body, not stuck on top of it.

When you look at a side view, you can see that the nose is very long on this type of character. Notice, too, that the neck does not attach to the base of the ear, but behind it. And yes, the neck really is that thick!

The lips stick out from the face.

Creating Bishie Characters

Make your leading men unique by including these Bishie traits.

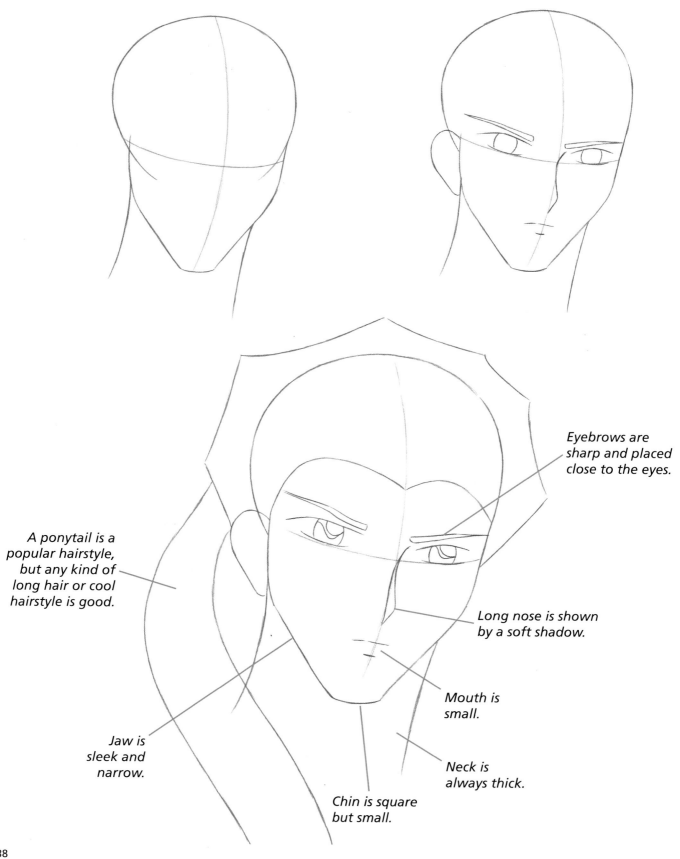

Eyebrows are sharp and placed close to the eyes.

A ponytail is a popular hairstyle, but any kind of long hair or cool hairstyle is good.

Long nose is shown by a soft shadow.

Mouth is small.

Jaw is sleek and narrow.

Neck is always thick.

Chin is square but small.

Drawing Eyes

The eyes of Japanese comic characters are famous, and shoujo eyes are the most brilliant, intense, and dazzling of all! Look at the leading man on page 139. What do his eyes tell you? What would they say if they were open wider or slitted? The eyes are the most detailed part of the face, so give yourself time to get them just right. You don't have to follow these examples exactly—draw the eyelashes differently, or create different shapes for the "shines" in the eyes or maybe even different eyebrows.

MALE EYES, FRONT VIEW

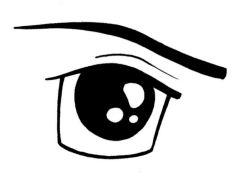

For young men and boys, the eyes are large and black, with multiple shines to make them look bright.

For men, including Bishies, the eyes have smaller eyeballs and a thinner shape.

Do you see the dots going around the pupil? That's the way we indicate the iris, the colored part of the eye.

FEMALE EYES, FRONT VIEW

Girl characters have wide-open eyes with lots of shines.

Women have almond-shaped eyes with feathery lashes.

This type of eye can be used for both young girls and women. For girls, make it bright; for women, add the extra line above the lashes.

In the side view, the basic shape of the eyes is the same for men and women. It changes for young and old characters, though.

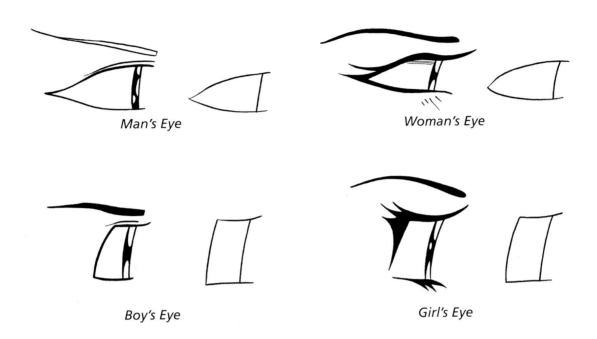

Man's Eye

Woman's Eye

Boy's Eye

Girl's Eye

Eyes, more than any other feature, show a shoujo character's personality. This girl is fun-loving yet thoughtful.

Here is the same girl in a side view. She has typical young female eyes—how would she look with different eyes? Try it!

Drawing the Female Body

Let your characters stand on their own two legs!
Look how the female body is made up of basic shapes
put together. Costumes cover these shapes, but your
characters will look better if you understand the forms
of each type of character—female, male, and Bishie.

FRONT VIEW
Most magical girls have
long legs and a narrow body.

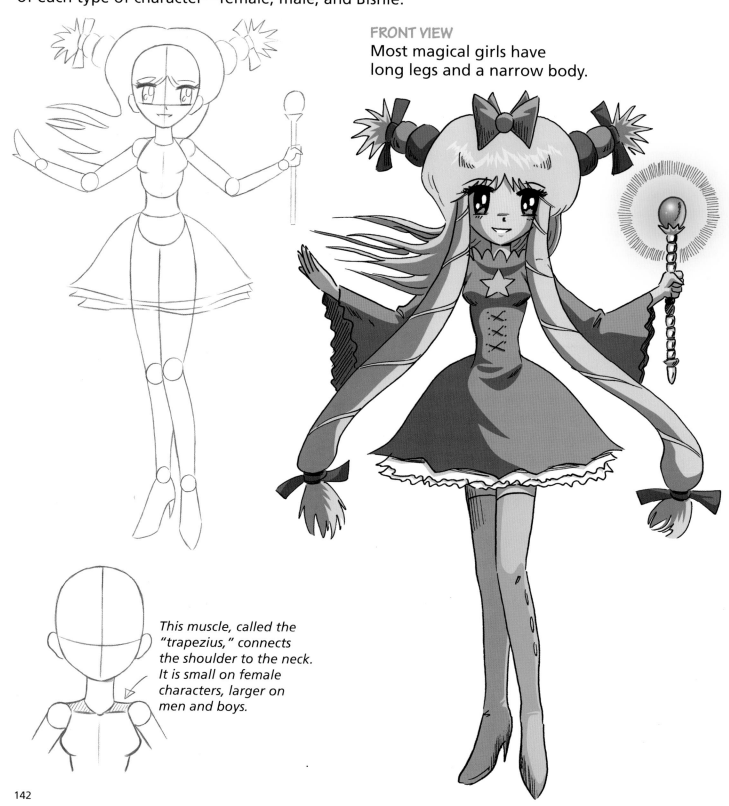

*This muscle, called the
"trapezius," connects
the shoulder to the neck.
It is small on female
characters, larger on
men and boys.*

Don't forget to draw both legs, even in the side view! You might be tempted to leave out the far leg, since it's hidden behind the front one. But that will look weird, as if one of her legs has disappeared. Instead, draw a hint of the far leg.

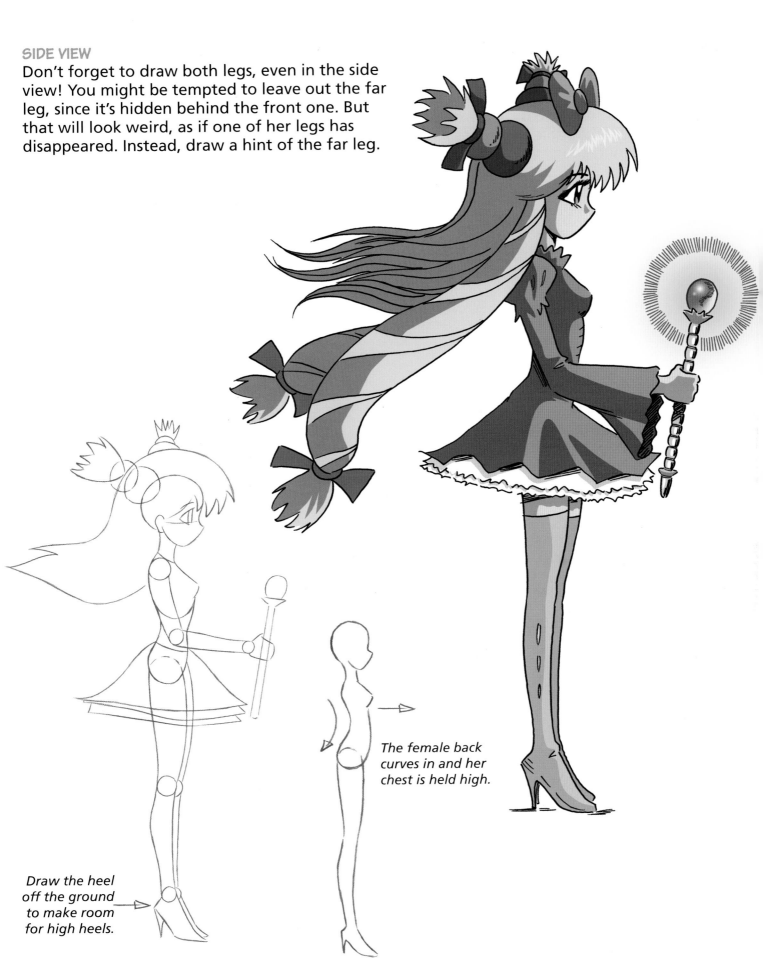

The female back curves in and her chest is held high.

Draw the heel off the ground to make room for high heels.

Drawing the Male Body

There are two different basic male shapes in shoujo: boys and Bishies. First let's look at how to draw teenagers or boys.

FRONT VIEW

Boys' chests are not much wider than their waists. Their arms can look a little muscular.

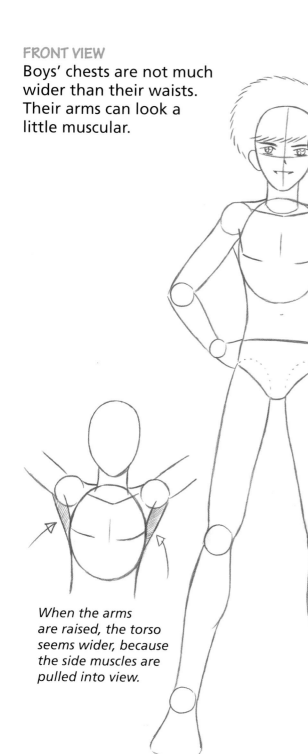

When the arms are raised, the torso seems wider, because the side muscles are pulled into view.

SIDE VIEW

In the side view, let the arms bend a bit at the elbow. If the arms are straight, the pose will look stiff and awkward.

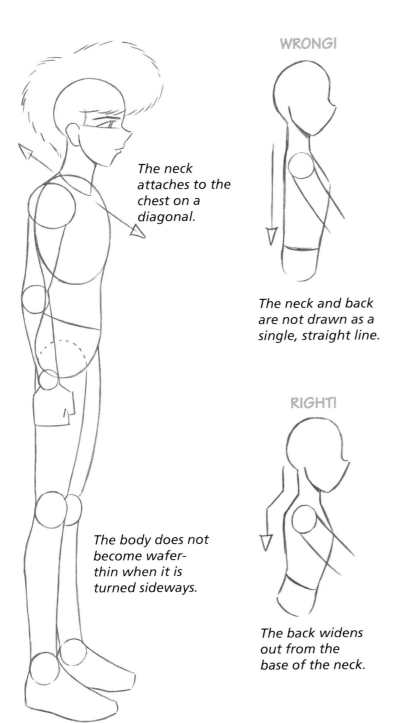

The neck attaches to the chest on a diagonal.

The body does not become wafer-thin when it is turned sideways.

WRONG!

The neck and back are not drawn as a single, straight line.

RIGHT!

The back widens out from the base of the neck.

Drawing the Bishie Body

Bishies are smooth. They can be regal and wealthy or cool and trendy. They are also cast as fantasy characters, such as knights. Many shoujo stories have a Bishie.

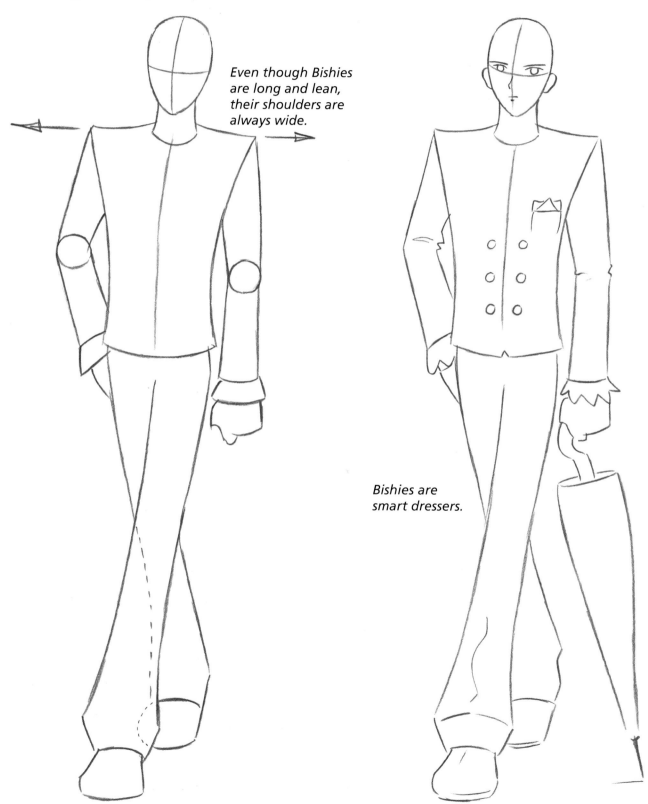

Even though Bishies are long and lean, their shoulders are always wide.

Bishies are smart dressers.

Drawing Seated Characters

The trick to drawing a character that's sitting down is to draw the chair first, *then* add the figure sitting on it. If you try to draw the character first, it will look weightless, as if the person is floating.

First draw the chair...

...then draw the girl sitting on the chair.

Drawing Hands

To draw real-looking hands, remember this: The knuckles and the fingers are drawn on an arch. Lightly sketch a curved line to help you draw the fingers and knuckles correctly.

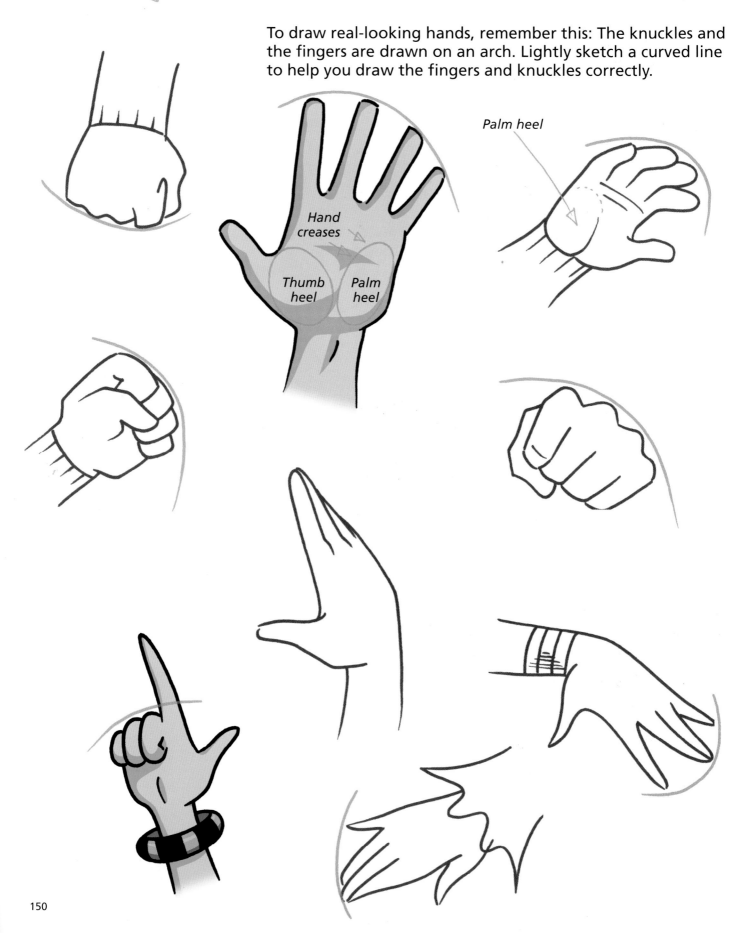

Palm heel

Hand creases

Thumb heel

Palm heel

Drawing Feet and Shoes

Feet are harder for people to draw than hands. Why? My guess is that people don't usually look at their own feet, but they always see and notice their own hands. Also, while the palm is almost flat, the foot has a built-in arch.

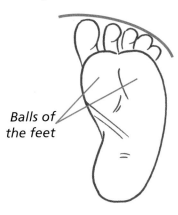

Balls of the feet

TOP VIEW
A shoe is shaped like a foot, but simpler.

BOTTOM VIEW
Like fingers, toes follow a curve. The bottom of the sneaker should have grip marks.

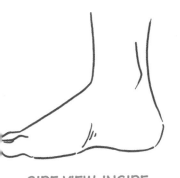

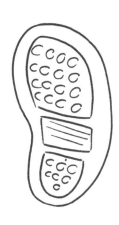

Toes are drawn along an arch.

SIDE VIEW, INSIDE
The sole of the shoe angles in at the arch, then back out again. Add lots of rubber to the soles of sneakers, as well as stripes on the sides.

SIDE VIEW, OUTSIDE
The shape of the outer side of the shoe also curves in at the midpoint and then out again, but not as much as on the other side.

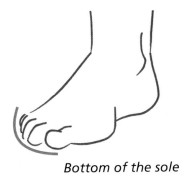

Bottom of the sole

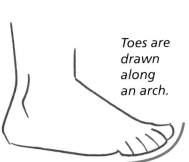

THREE-QUARTER VIEW
In this view, you should see a little bit of the bottom of the sole.

Front half of shoe overlaps the back of the shoe.

SCHOOL COMICS

Now that you've mastered the basics, it's time for the exciting part: creating great characters! Let's start with school comics, which focus on the adventures of school-age teens, and are among the most popular types of shoujo. If you can draw the core characters, you're on your way to creating your own comics!

Uniforms for Girls

First, let's look at school uniforms. In the United States, kids in school wear jeans, T-shirts, whatever they like. But in Japan, girls and boys are required to wear uniforms. So shoujo characters wear these outfits in school...but after school, and on weekends, they can wear anything they like. Here are some typical uniforms for girls. Skirts are just above the knee, and shirts have high necklines.

SWEATER AND SKIRT

SAILOR OUTFIT

BLOUSE AND SKIRT

SAILOR OUTFIT WITH SCARF

Uniforms for Boys

Boys' uniforms can be a simple suit, a neat sweater and trousers, or a trendy jacket and pants.

JACKET AND TIE

SWEATER AND PANTS

NEHRU JACKET

SHORT JACKET

Student Athlete

A student athlete is a staple of school comics. You don't have to draw fancy moves or extreme poses—all that's needed is a team uniform, athletic shoes, and a ball.

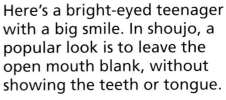

Here's a bright-eyed teenager with a big smile. In shoujo, a popular look is to leave the open mouth blank, without showing the teeth or tongue.

The leg in back is much shorter than the front leg. That's because we're looking down on her from above.

Bangs are always close to the eyes.

BOWS, JEWELS, AND FLOWERS

Shoujo artists like to embellish their work with graceful decorations. Here are some extras you can use for your characters.

Joe Cool

Okay, so he's vain and self-centered. Readers still love characters like this, and so do all of the schoolgirl characters in shoujo! Note the stylish crew-neck shirt with the open jacket—very trendy.

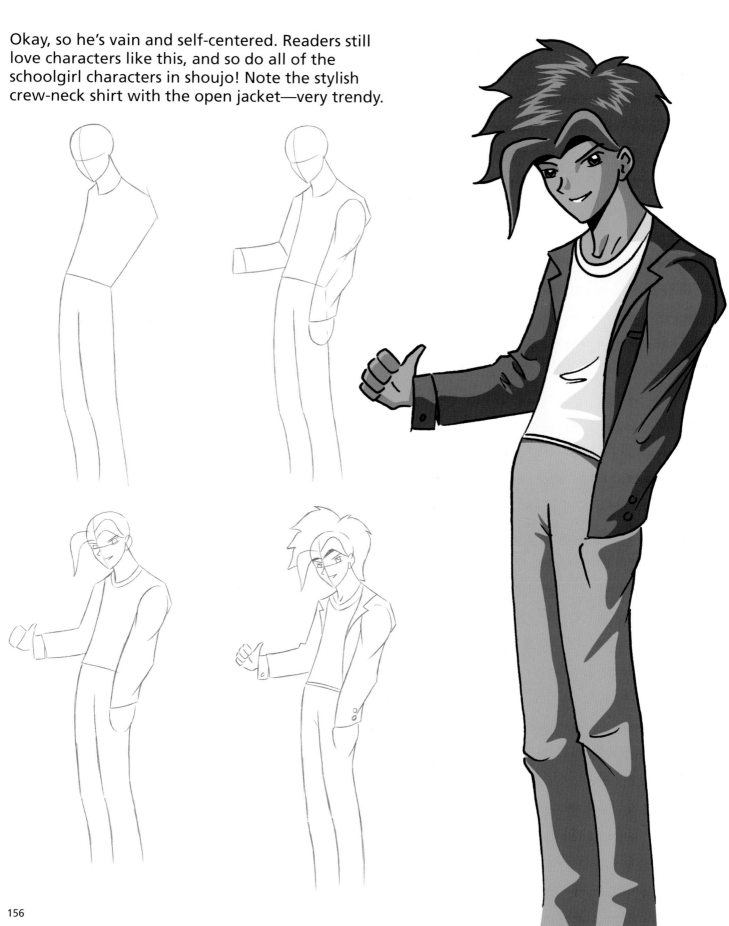

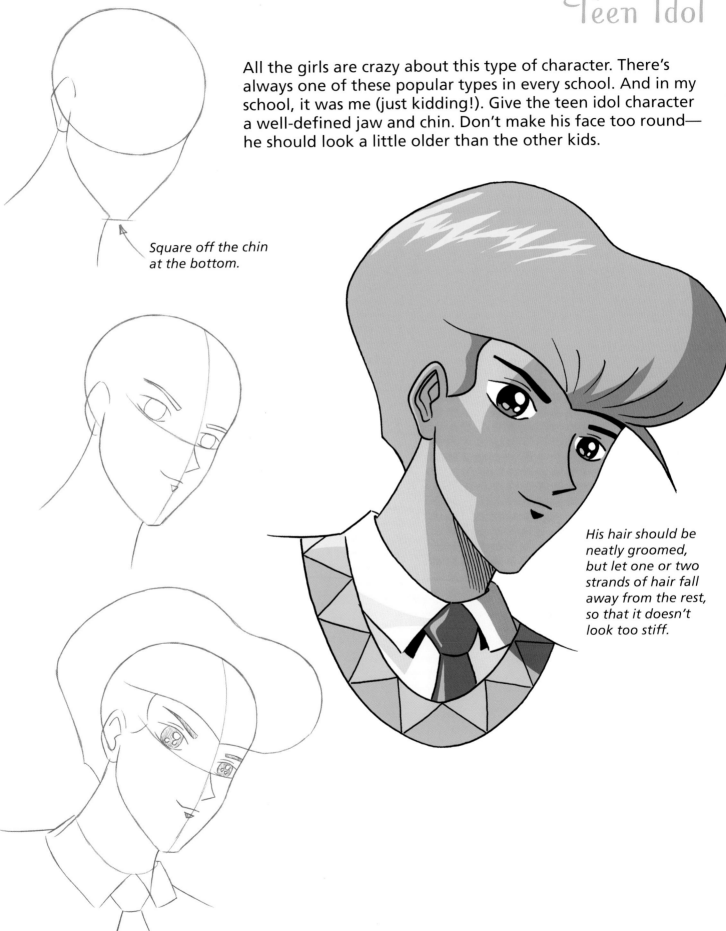

All the girls are crazy about this type of character. There's always one of these popular types in every school. And in my school, it was me (just kidding!). Give the teen idol character a well-defined jaw and chin. Don't make his face too round— he should look a little older than the other kids.

Square off the chin at the bottom.

His hair should be neatly groomed, but let one or two strands of hair fall away from the rest, so that it doesn't look too stiff.

Lunch Break

Time for a picnic lunch. To create a casual mood, this schoolboy's jacket is open, and the sleeves are rolled up. His crossed legs are easy to draw, because you don't have to show his feet!

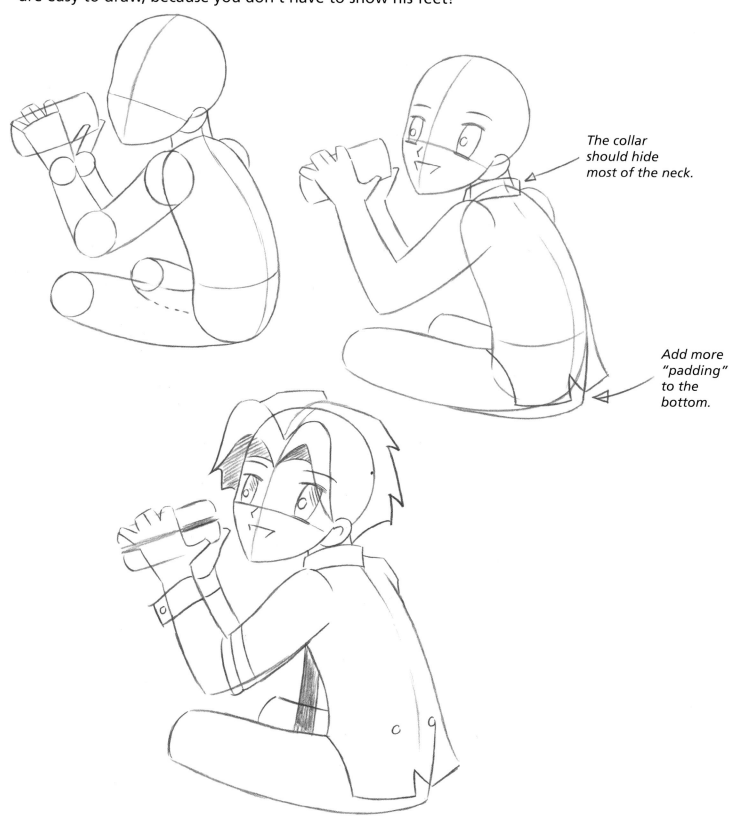

The collar should hide most of the neck.

Add more "padding" to the bottom.

Backpack Boy

Nehru jackets are popular, and since the shape of the jacket is basically a rectangle, you can just draw a rectangle for the upper body. Easy! The trademark of the Nehru jacket is the high collar. Give the boy a center part and wild hair sticking up from the back.

Sidewalk Racer

See how the pose makes her look as if she's really riding the skateboard? What makes this pose so convincing? The arms? They're important—but the key is the way she's bending her knees in. Also, she bends a bit at the waist. In action poses, the worst thing you can do is make your character stiff. Keep her loose and flexible!

MAGIC TIME

Some of the coolest characters in shoujo are the beings with special powers—magical girls and boys, goddesses and demigods, fantasy fighters, princesses, fairies, elves, and many more. Learning to draw these characters will add excitement to your manga shoujo!

Magical Girls

Magical girls take school comics one step further. Most of the time, these characters are ordinary schoolgirls. But when faced with injustice and evil, they use secret powers to transform themselves into powerful fighters to defeat the forces of darkness. Their costumes are often based on school uniforms.

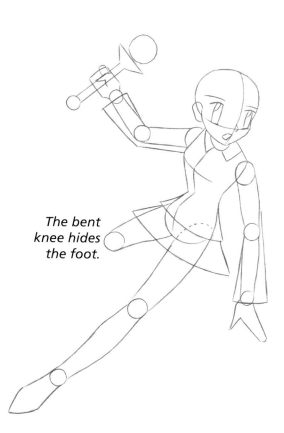

The bent knee hides the foot.

When a magical girl carries a wand or other magical instrument, it's a good chance to use special effects, like these energy lines and sparkles.

Magical Girl with Cape

Here's a fancy magical girl character. To make it easy, I've broken it down into six simple steps. The hair, in the last step, makes it look hard. But actually, that's the easiest part—you can draw the hair differently than I do, and it will be a hairstyle you invented!

Boots with high heels look futuristic.

Fantasy Fighter

Sword in hand, the fantasy fighter is ready to take on the beasts of the netherworld! Note the long, flowing locks—and how about those cool swirls of hair on the sides of her head? Bracelets on the upper arm are used only for fantasy characters.

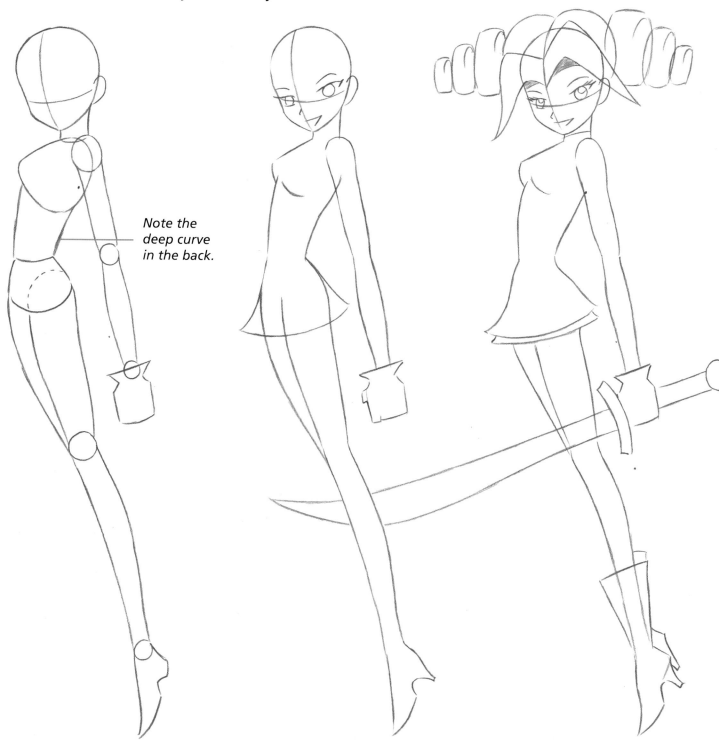

Note the deep curve in the back.

Hero Girl

This magical girl strikes a heroic pose as she defends her people against the lords of darkness and evil. Notice how she shows her enemies (yes, she's usually outnumbered!) that she is ready to fight. Her legs are in the classic flying position.

Ignore her tiara and hair rings, and she's no more difficult to draw than any other girl character.

Even though she is clearly a fantasy character, her outfit is based on the typical sailor school uniform.

Magical Boy

Like the magical girl, the magical boy also puts on a souped-up costume to battle the bad guys. A cape with a high collar adds a dramatic touch.

When objects overlap, "draw through" with very light lines to get the placement right.

Intergalactic fighters appear all the time in shoujo. In science fiction, you'll often find two different ideas mixed together—for example, this character's uniform looks like something from the future; maybe it's the jacket of a soldier in a royal space force. Yet his weapon is low-tech: a simple sword. Combining the past with the future is a great way to create cool sci-fi manga characters.

Boy with Special Powers

Boys with special powers fight on the same side as magical girls. These boys don't have to change costumes, the way the magical girls and boys do. They often have mystical weapons. But don't let the magic sword do all the work for you! You still need to draw a good pose. A cool martial arts stance works well for fight scenes.

Gallant Knight

Bishies make great medieval heroes. But don't put them in armor. They are much more dramatic when costumed in wide-collar shirts with puffed-out sleeves, a sash at the waist, and high boots.

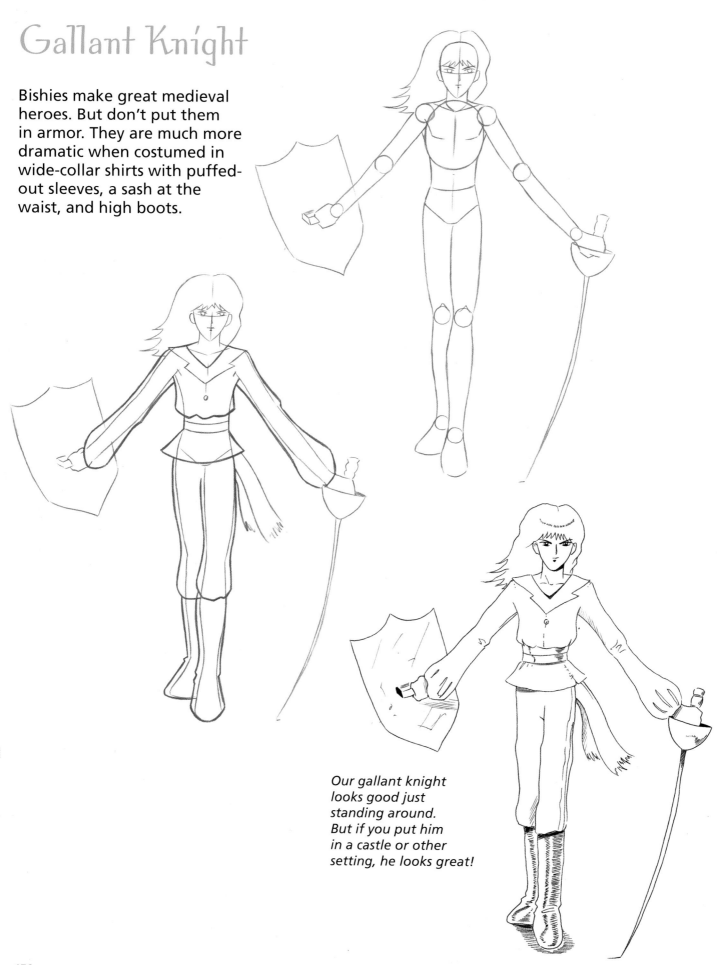

Our gallant knight looks good just standing around. But if you put him in a castle or other setting, he looks great!

Demigod

Demigods and their female counterparts, goddesses, are very appealing. Ethereal beings, they can appear and disappear at will. They use their tremendous power wisely, and they are always drawn as if they are floating above the ground.

SIMPLIFYING FOLDS
To draw a flowing hem on a robe, just follow these three steps.

1. First, draw a squiggly line with hills and valleys.

2. Connect lines to the tops of the hills.

3. Add lines to the bottoms of the valleys.

Goddess

To make a goddess, all you have to do is draw a pretty woman, make the hair and the dress longer, and add wings.

The ponytail on top of the head is always a good look for goddess characters.

FAIRIES AND FRIENDS

Some of the best-loved characters of shoujo are the enchanted beings, with their delicate, beautiful features and expressive eyes. These magical spirits of nature are most often on the side of good.

Fairy Girl

Young fairies have wide faces with very large eyes that show innocence and honesty. The almond-shaped eyes should be tilted up at the ends.

Fantasy Princess

Princesses are always pretty, and this character is no exception. The cone-shaped headpieces on either side of her head resemble the buns that were worn by the upper classes in the Middle Ages. The tiara shows that she is of noble birth.

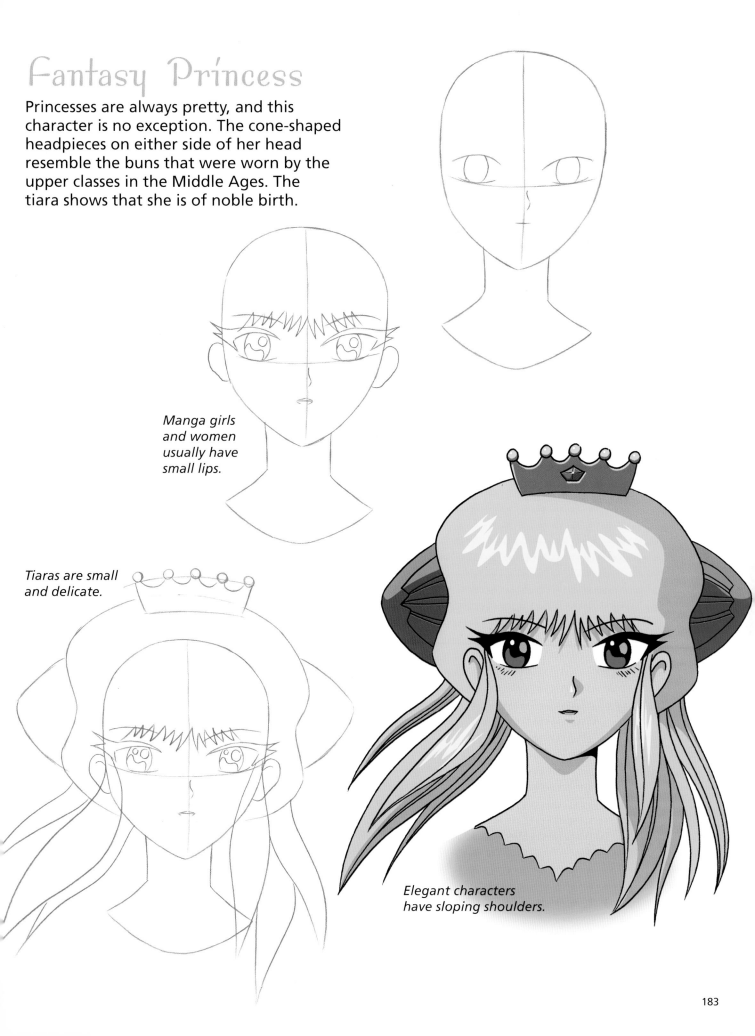

Manga girls and women usually have small lips.

Tiaras are small and delicate.

Elegant characters have sloping shoulders.

Elfin Queen

The fancy cones, jeweled choker, and long, flowing hair give this elfin queen a graceful quality, as do her beautiful eyes. The ears are very long, in the shoujo style of fairies and elves.

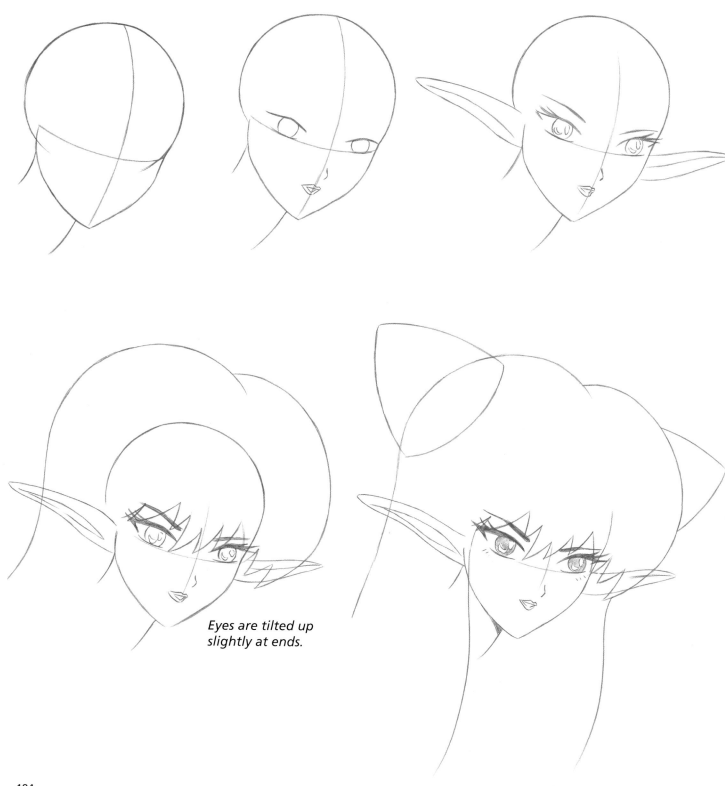

Eyes are tilted up slightly at ends.

Flying Fairy

Fairies are creatures of earth and nature, and so their clothing should look natural—nothing too fancy. In fact, fairies can even go barefoot. Fairy wings are not drawn with feathers, but like the wings of a bee.

Fantasy characters can wear special jewelry like this thigh bracelet.

Kids Draw
MANGA FANTASY

Manga Fantasy Basics 190

DRAWING FANTASY BOY FACES
DRAWING FANTASY GIRL FACES
DESIGNING HAIR
DRAWING THE POWER FIST
DRAWING SPECTACULAR EYES

DRAWING THE NECK
DRAWING THE MALE BODY
DRAWING THE FEMALE BODY
CREATING A NATURAL-LOOKING POSE

Fairies and Knights 202

FAIRY PRINCESS
FAIRY SORCERER
STANDING FAIRY
FAIRY AND BABY

FANTASY KNIGHT
HEROIC KNIGHT
KNIGHTS AND CASTLES

Flying Characters 216

DRAWING WINGS
ADVANCED FANTASY-WING WORKSHOP
FANTASY GUARDIAN

WINGED FANTASY ANGEL
FAIRIES IN FLIGHT

Magical Effects 224

CREATING THREADS OF MAGIC
THE MAGICAL STAFF

MAGICAL WEAPONS
POWER PACKS

Supernatural Beings 234

HUMAN-ANIMAL CHARACTERS
WIZARDS AND WARLOCKS
MERMAIDS OF THE DEEP
DEMON BEAST

MYSTERIOUS ORB
AWESOME CHARACTER
THE CHALLENGE DRAWING

MANGA FANTASY BASICS

Ready to have some fun? Let's start with the basics, and then we'll build on your skills. Soon you'll be creating your own amazing fantasy characters!

Drawing Fantasy Boy Faces

The basic teen boy's face is soft, not angular—except for the chin, which is delicate and pointed. The eyes of fantasy boy characters are big, but not huge, as they are on some manga characters.

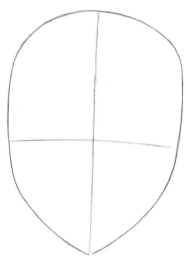

Draw light lines to guide you, then erase them at the end.

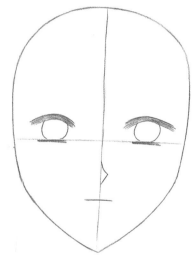

Make the upper eyelids thicker than the lower eyelids.

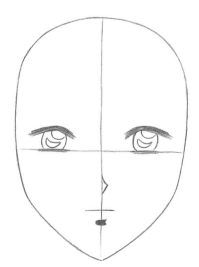

Add a small shadow under the lip.

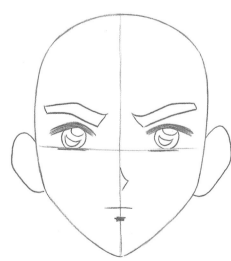

Draw thick eyebrows.

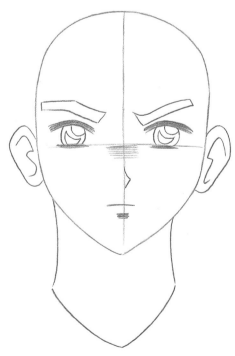

Give him an athletic neck (heroes never have skinny necks).

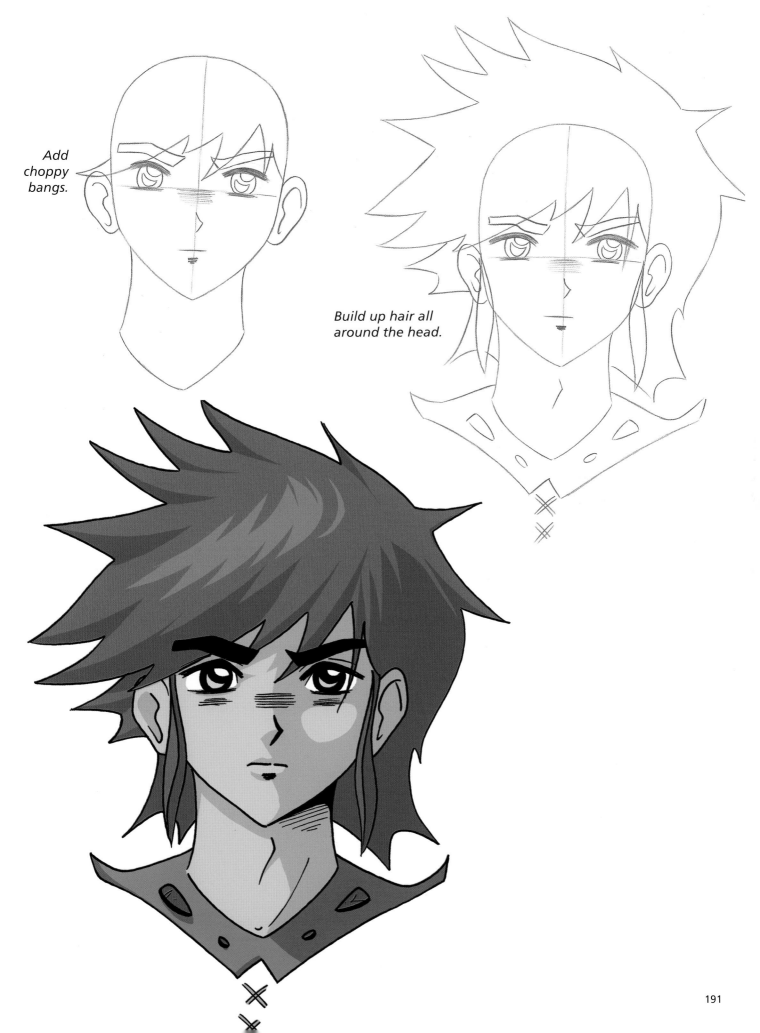

Add choppy bangs.

Build up hair all around the head.

Drawing Fantasy Girl Faces

The female face begins with the same soft shape as the male head but the jawline is a little fuller around the cheeks.

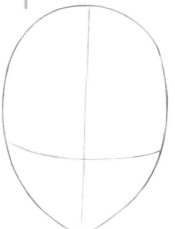

Draw guidelines for the eyes and the center of the face

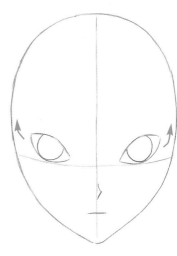

Tilt the eyes up at the ends, for an enchanted look.

Make the eyebrows sharp, and point them down slightly.

Add small and dainty lips.

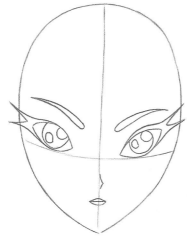

Draw the eyelashes thick and dark.

Make the ear really stick ou

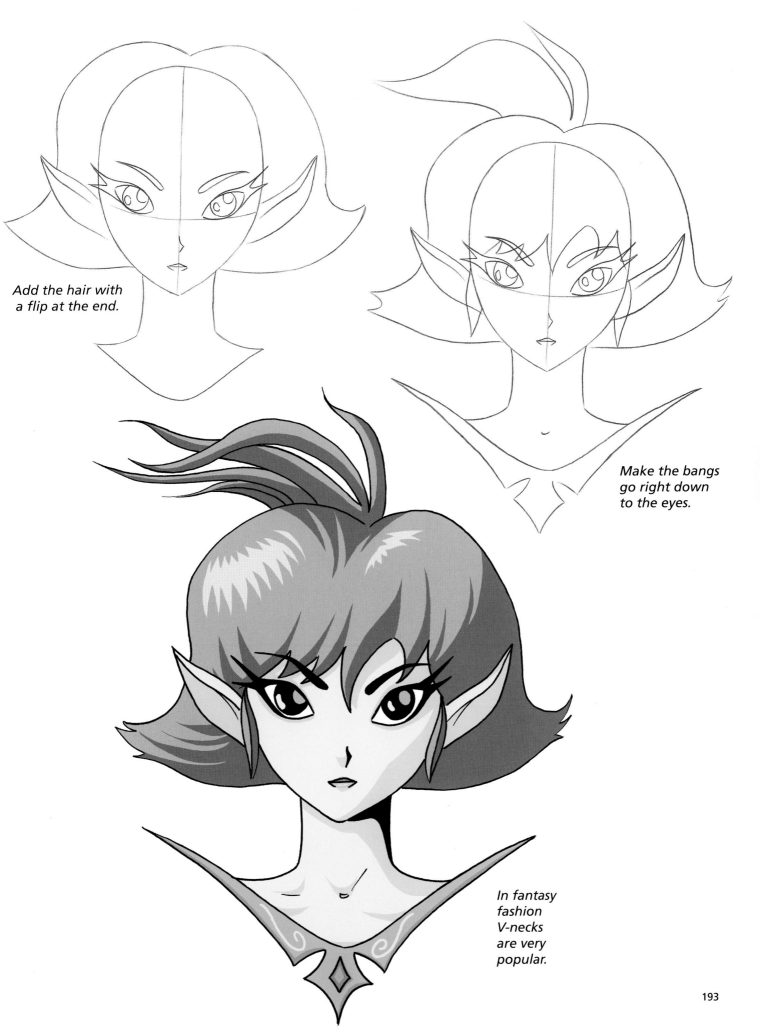

Add the hair with a flip at the end.

Make the bangs go right down to the eyes.

In fantasy fashion V-necks are very popular.

Designing Hair

It's fun to draw wild and stylish hairdos on your character. But the tricky part comes when you have to draw where the hairline meets the scalp. You need to know where the natural hairline falls on a character's head.

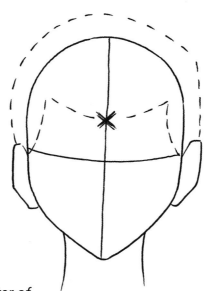

The "X" marks the center of the head, where a "middle part" would start. Manga characters always have big hair—it never lies flat.

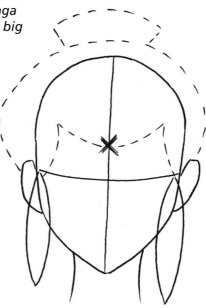

CREATING SPIKY HAIR

Spiky hair is a classic feature of manga characters. The secret to drawing it is simple— make sure that all of the spikes travel in the same direction!

RIGHT
The spikes of the hair all travel in the same direction.

WRONG
The spikes of the hair travel in different directions.

In fantasy manga the fist is the most dynamic hand pose. A character can raise it in anger, grip an object or a weapon with it, or use it to punch a bad guy's lights out! As you can see below, there are many angles from which we can draw the fist.

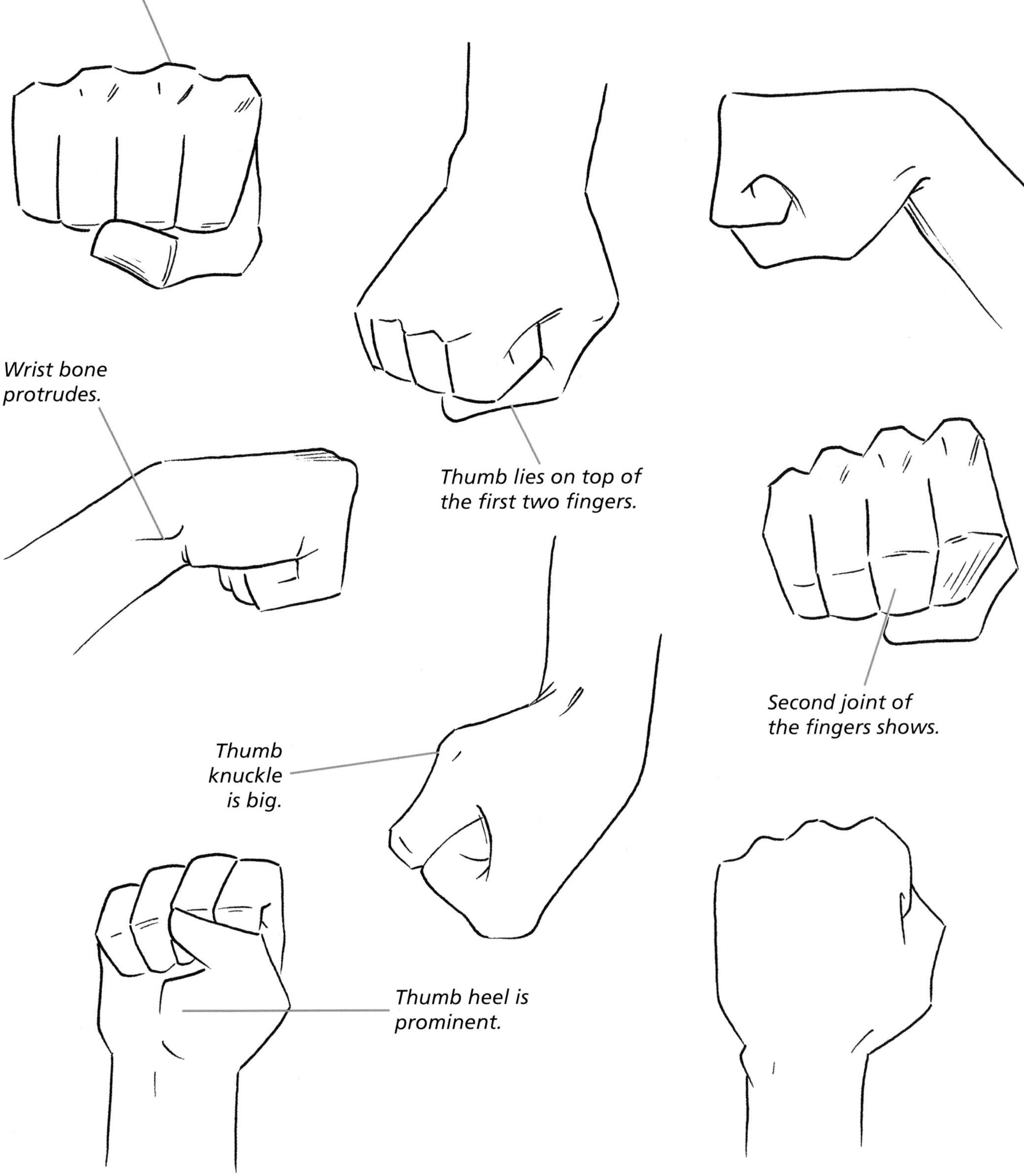

Each knuckle appears in the middle of the finger.

Wrist bone protrudes.

Thumb lies on top of the first two fingers.

Thumb knuckle is big.

Thumb heel is prominent.

Second joint of the fingers shows.

Drawing Spectacular Eyes

Manga characters are famous for their sparkling eyes with giant "shines" inside them—the shine is light reflecting off the dark parts of the eye. The trick is to create patterns and designs within the eye, and not just a plain circle for a shine. Check out these examples, and then try drawing your own.

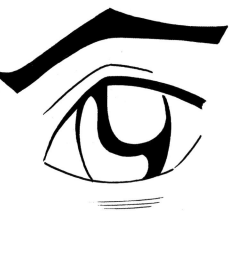

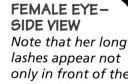

FEMALE EYE—SIDE VIEW
Note that her long lashes appear not only in front of the eye, but behind the eye as well.

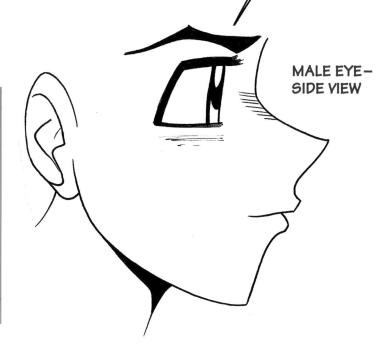

MALE EYE—SIDE VIEW

CLOSED EYES
There are three basic expressions caused by closed eyes:

HAPPY
The eyes curve down.

SHY
The eyes curve up.

ANGRY OR SAD
The eyes tilt down, toward the nose.

Drawing the Neck

Beginners often draw the neck straight up and down. This is a mistake—but one that you'll now be able to avoid. Draw the neck at an angle instead. It'll look much more natural.

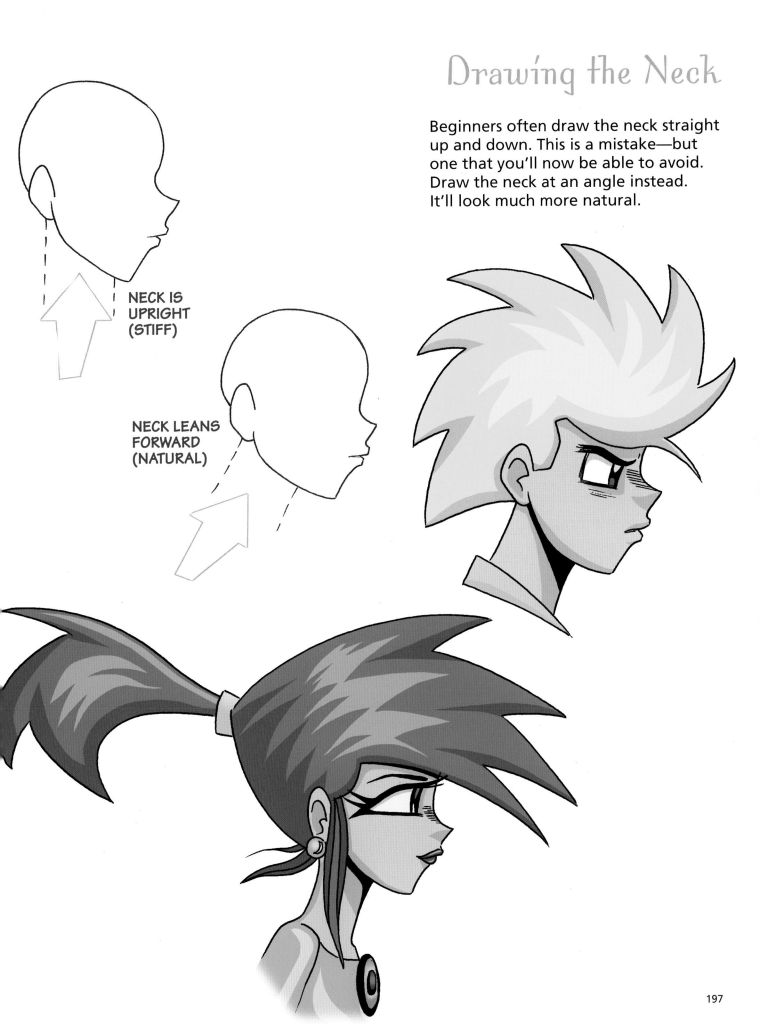

NECK IS
UPRIGHT
(STIFF)

NECK LEANS
FORWARD
(NATURAL)

Drawing the Male Body

When drawing the body, there are some simple, but little known, tricks you can use to make sure your proportions are correct. Take a look at the labels, and you'll see that it's easy!

FRONT VIEW

SIDE VIEW

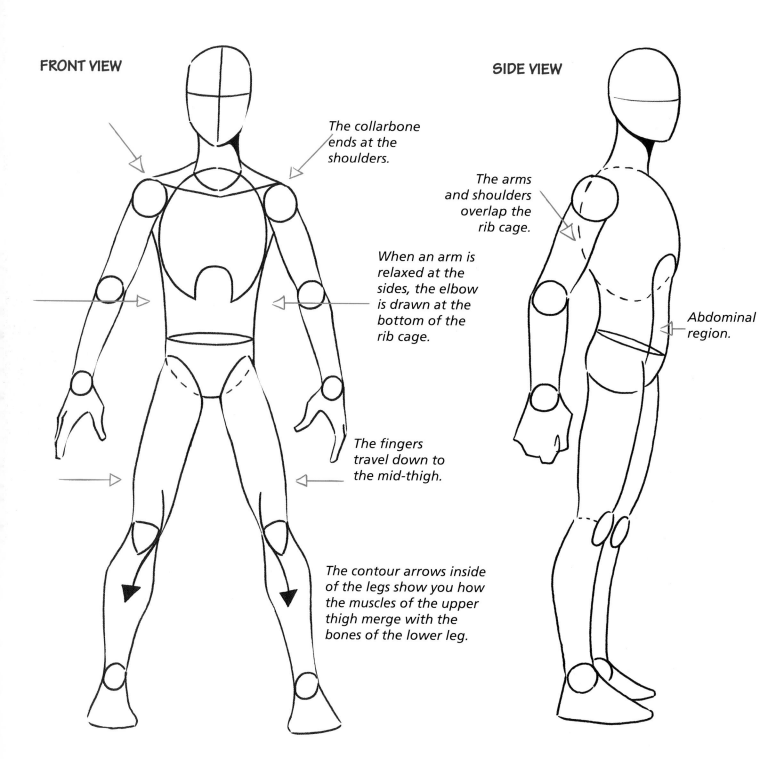

The collarbone ends at the shoulders.

The arms and shoulders overlap the rib cage.

When an arm is relaxed at the sides, the elbow is drawn at the bottom of the rib cage.

Abdominal region.

The fingers travel down to the mid-thigh.

The contour arrows inside of the legs show you how the muscles of the upper thigh merge with the bones of the lower leg.

Many beginners draw the body with straight lines—but this is a mistake. The body is dynamic. It has lots of curves, even on limbs that have fairly straight bones.

BODY DRAWN WITH STRAIGHT LINES (WRONG)
Straight lines make the body look stiff and awkward.

BODY DRAWN WITH CURVED LINES (RIGHT)
Curved lines make the body look natural and lifelike.

Drawing the Female Body

The female figure can be challenging to draw. But it's much easier if we simply divide the torso into three parts: chest, midsection, and hips. Note that the shoulders and hips are equally wide, giving the female figure an "hourglass" look.

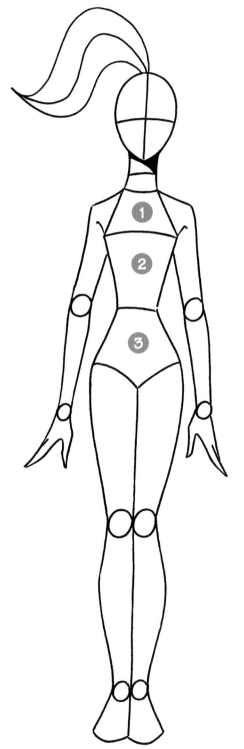

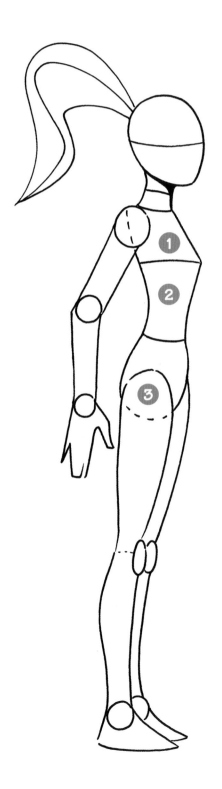

Creating a Natural-Looking Pose

The secret to making a pose look natural is simple: put more of the weight on one leg than the other. Many beginning artists draw their characters with equal weight on both legs. But who stands like that, other than soldiers in the army? No one.

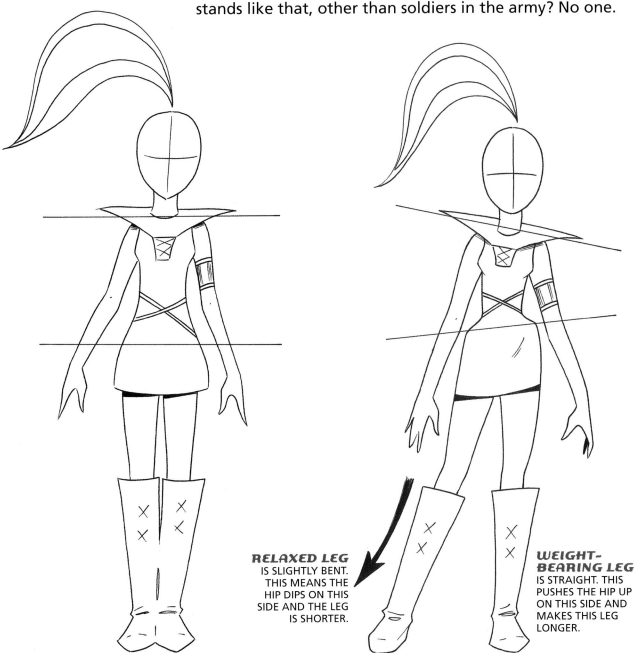

RELAXED LEG IS SLIGHTLY BENT. THIS MEANS THE HIP DIPS ON THIS SIDE AND THE LEG IS SHORTER.

WEIGHT-BEARING LEG IS STRAIGHT. THIS PUSHES THE HIP UP ON THIS SIDE AND MAKES THIS LEG LONGER.

EQUAL WEIGHT PLACED ON BOTH LEGS

Both legs have equal weight on them. That means that the shoulders and hips are straight, parallel to the floor. See how stiff the pose looks?

NATURAL-LOOKING POSE

The leg that is directly underneath the body bears most of the weight. The relaxed leg moves away from the body, with the knee slightly bent. This causes the shoulders and the hips to tilt at opposing angles.

FAIRIES AND KNIGHTS

Now that you know the basics, it's time to create your very own fantasy characters!

Fairy Princess

Princesses are always charming and captivating. When you see one, you know something magical and wondrous is in the air. We'll start with a "medium shot," which means from the waist up. The medium shot is very effective, because we can get the full feeling of the character without the complexity of drawing the entire figure.

Natural curve of spine

Dip chin down into shoulder for a mysterious look.

DRAWING THE FAIRY EYE

The eye of the fairy is different from that of other manga characters. It tilts up at the ends, even more than on a regular female character. The eye is also narrower, and the eyelashes, as well as the eyebrow, are sharper. The eyeball itself is tucked deeper into the upper eyelid, adding a mysterious touch.

REGULAR FEMALE EYE
The regular female eye has a bigger eyeball.

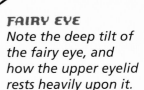

FAIRY EYE
Note the deep tilt of the fairy eye, and how the upper eyelid rests heavily upon it.

Magical jewels and crystals are a popular part of the manga fantasy genre. These jewels bestow special powers upon the holder, and are therefore sought by many—especially those with evil aspirations.

203

Fairy Sorcerer

Is he good or evil? That's for you to decide, for he is a powerful being who uses magic for his own purposes. Give him a sleek face and pointy chin. And if you want to make him look extra-sinister (which I do!), give him tiny eyebrows and a long, slim nose.

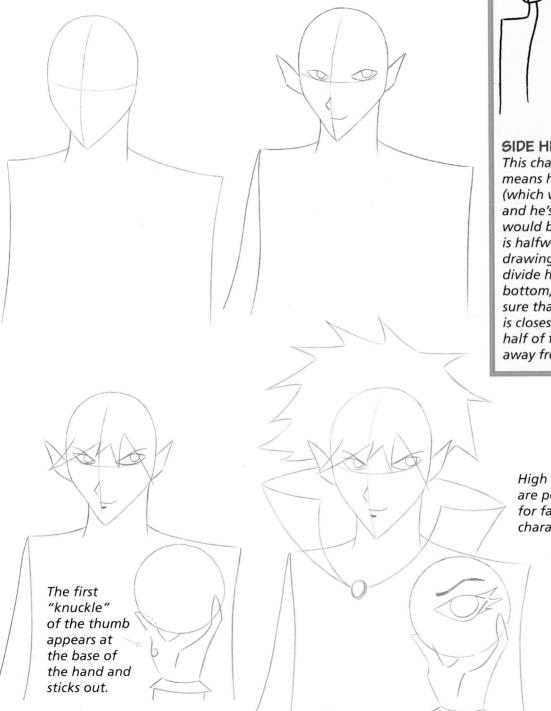

CLOSER HALF OF BODY IS ALWAYS LARGER IN THE 3/4 VIEW

SIDE HINT

This character is in a 3/4 view. That means he's not facing directly at us (which would be a "front view"), and he's not facing sideways (which would be a "profile"). Instead, he is halfway between the two. When drawing a character in a 3/4 view, divide him in half, from top to bottom, with a "center line." Make sure that the half of the body that is closest to you is larger than the half of the body that is furthest away from you.

High collars are popular for fantasy characters.

The first "knuckle" of the thumb appears at the base of the hand and sticks out.

Standing Fairy

Drawing a fairy standing in a sweeping breeze makes her look very appealing. Remember to first sketch the torso by dividing it into three parts, then draw her body with lots of curving lines. And to make the pose more dramatic, try combining two different angles: draw her body turned at a 3/4 angle, but have her head face us at a front angle.

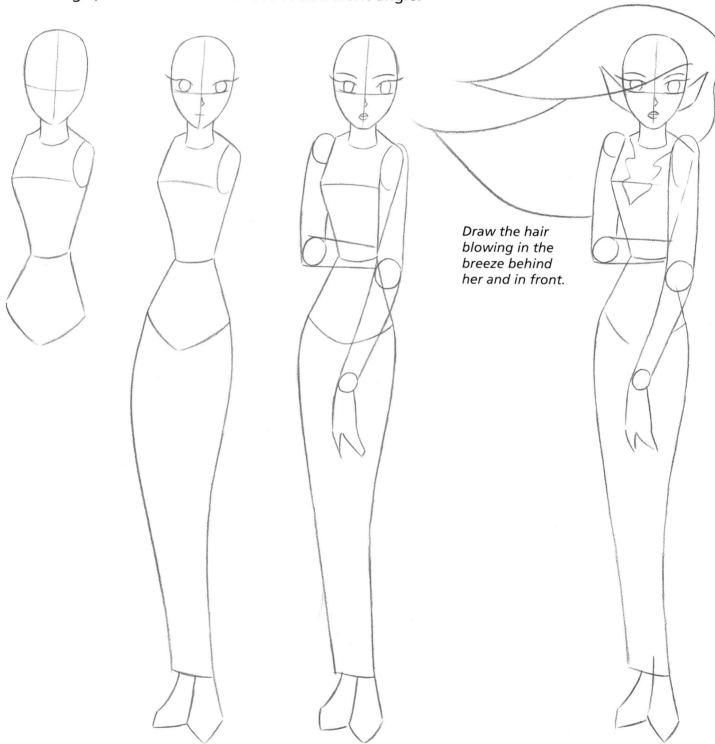

Draw the hair blowing in the breeze behind her and in front.

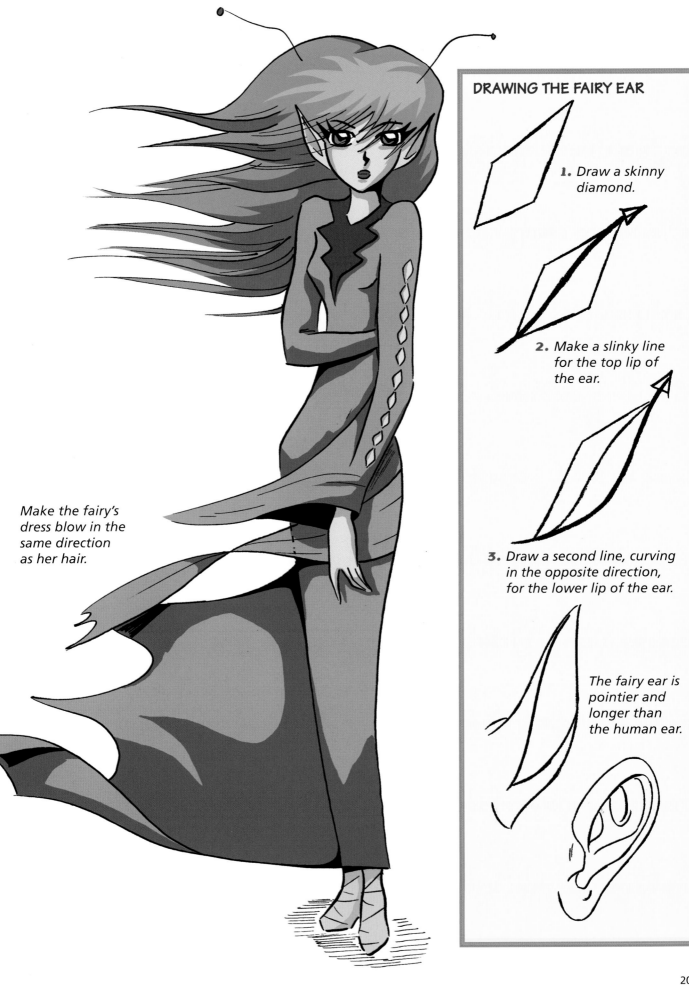

Make the fairy's dress blow in the same direction as her hair.

DRAWING THE FAIRY EAR

1. Draw a skinny diamond.

2. Make a slinky line for the top lip of the ear.

3. Draw a second line, curving in the opposite direction, for the lower lip of the ear.

The fairy ear is pointier and longer than the human ear.

Fairy and Baby

Fairies are attentive mothers and always keep their children close to them. They need to protect them from the many dangers that lurk in the forest. Charmed creatures, predatory animals, and evil spirits abound. But through it all, the magic of the fairy world keeps shining.

The line of the backpack doubles as the line of her upper arm!

The back has a feminine, sweeping curve to it.

MALE VERSUS FEMALE HIPS

Female hips slant forward, at an angle, while male hips are much straighter.

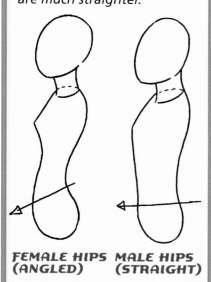

FEMALE HIPS (ANGLED) **MALE HIPS (STRAIGHT)**

The tummy sticks out just a touch, caused by the hips slanting forward.

Two small hands are all that's needed for a baby fairy— the arms don't show at this angle.

Fantasy Knight

Knights are especially popular in fantasy-based manga. They are often portrayed with special powers and possess fantasy weapons. But no matter how you design your fantasy character, it all begins with the basic knight costume.

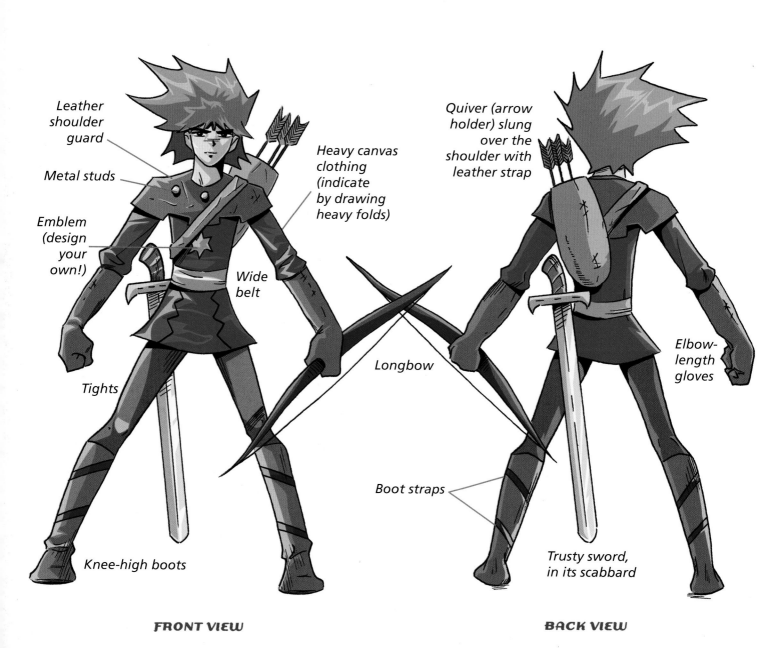

Leather shoulder guard

Metal studs

Emblem (design your own!)

Tights

Knee-high boots

Heavy canvas clothing (indicate by drawing heavy folds)

Wide belt

Longbow

Quiver (arrow holder) slung over the shoulder with leather strap

Elbow-length gloves

Boot straps

Trusty sword, in its scabbard

FRONT VIEW

BACK VIEW

Heroic Knight

Sword in hand, the heroic knight is ready to defend good against evil. His torch lights the way as he bravely enters the dangerous caves in the mountains of the green dragons.

Make the cuffs of the gloves oval.

HOW TO "DRAW THROUGH" AN OBJECT

Imagine an islander is holding a decorative pole in his hand. "Drawing through" the object means that we sketch the entire pole, even the part that will be hidden by his hand. In this way, we will be able to keep the pole straight.

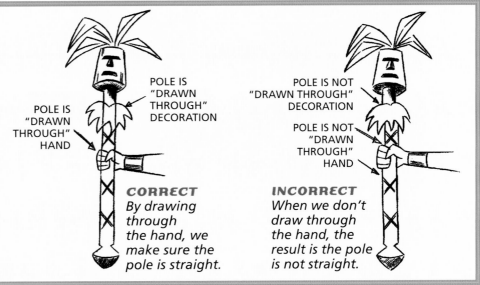

POLE IS "DRAWN THROUGH" HAND

POLE IS "DRAWN THROUGH" DECORATION

CORRECT
By drawing through the hand, we make sure the pole is straight.

POLE IS NOT "DRAWN THROUGH" DECORATION

POLE IS NOT "DRAWN THROUGH" HAND

INCORRECT
When we don't draw through the hand, the result is the pole is not straight.

Knights and Castles

Backgrounds can really liven up a scene. They ground it in time and place. Many beginning artists draw the characters on one spot on the page and the background objects on another. That's good in theory. But in practice, it's not so good. It usually leaves an empty space between the character and the background object.

The trick is to have the characters OVERLAP the background. That makes the character one with the scene and creates a feeling of depth.

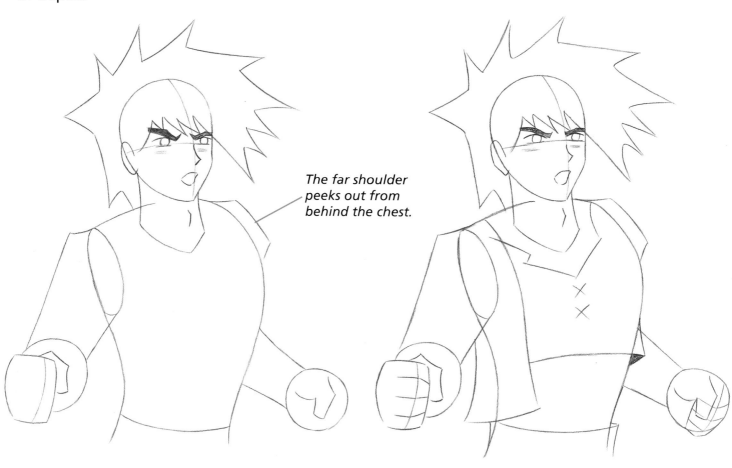

The far shoulder peeks out from behind the chest.

FLYING CHARACTERS

Winged beings are really popular in fantasy manga. They can be male or female and take the form of anything from angels to magical guardians to warriors.

Drawing Wings

The most common type of wing is the feathered wing. Many beginners know how to draw a simple wing. But very few know the trick to creating fantasy wings. So stay tuned while I open up the vault and pull out another secret technique.

ONLY OKAY
The bottom, feathered part slants inward, toward the body. Not a great look.

BETTER
By slanting the feathered part outward, you create a more graceful look.

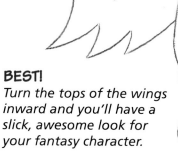

BEST!
Turn the tops of the wings inward and you'll have a slick, awesome look for your fantasy character.

Advanced Fantasy-Wing Workshop

In addition to the feathered wing, there are four other types of fantasy wings. Each one conveys a different feeling, so you can use them to show the personality of your fantasy character.

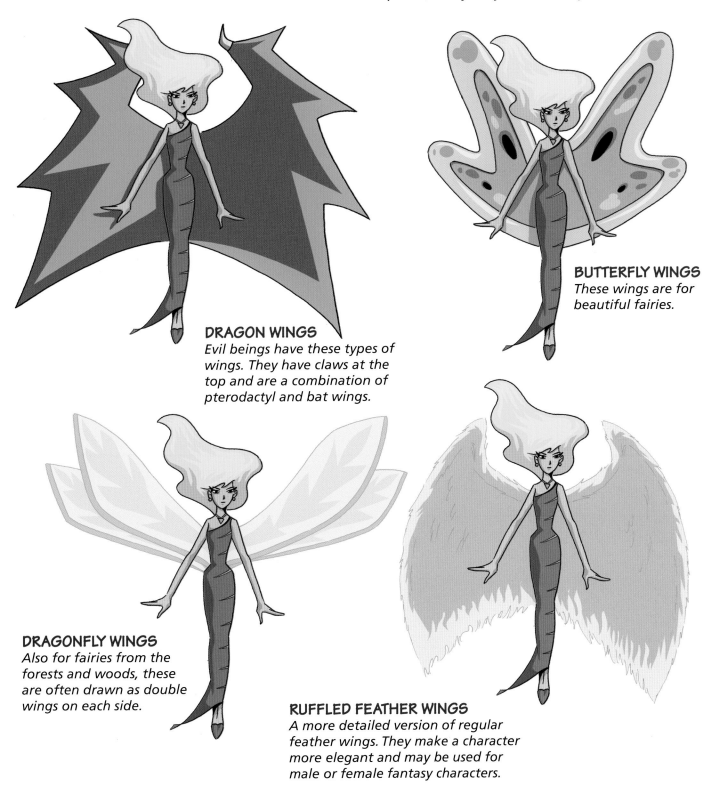

DRAGON WINGS
Evil beings have these types of wings. They have claws at the top and are a combination of pterodactyl and bat wings.

BUTTERFLY WINGS
These wings are for beautiful fairies.

DRAGONFLY WINGS
Also for fairies from the forests and woods, these are often drawn as double wings on each side.

RUFFLED FEATHER WINGS
A more detailed version of regular feather wings. They make a character more elegant and may be used for male or female fantasy characters.

Fantasy Guardian

The fantasy guardian is a serene being, but when called to action, he can instantly transform into a fearless fighter. He usually dresses in a fantasy prince outfit and has long, flowing hair.

Draw a head small in comparison to the body. This makes your character look even taller.

Give him wide shoulders.

A puffy-sleeved shirt like the ones musketeers wear is a good look.

Fantasy characters often wear high boots.

Sweep the hair dramatically to one side.

Add the wings.

Winged Fantasy Angel

Fantasy angels are always tranquil and beautiful. This charming pose shows one sitting on her knees, facing forward.

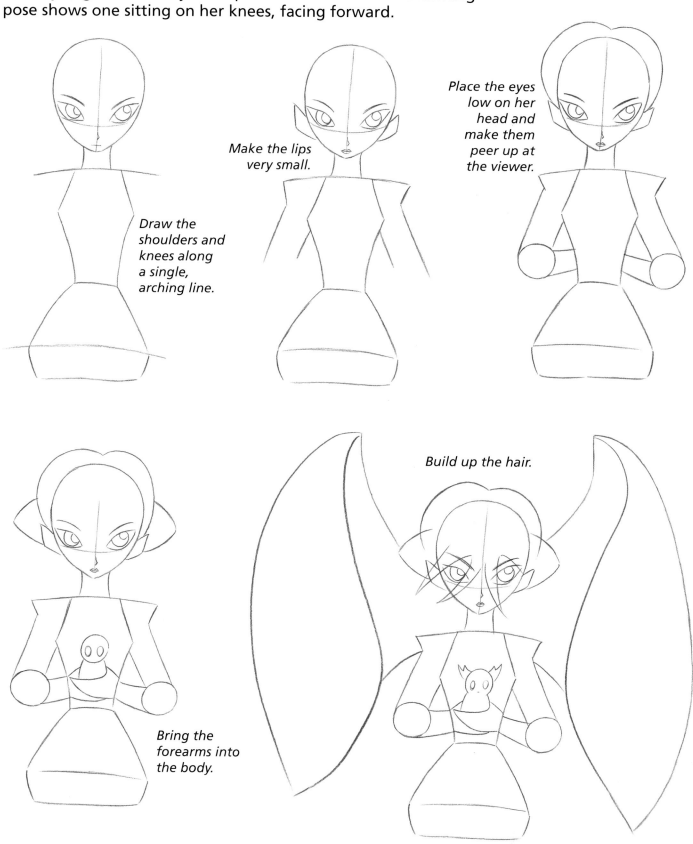

Draw the shoulders and knees along a single, arching line.

Make the lips very small.

Place the eyes low on her head and make them peer up at the viewer.

Bring the forearms into the body.

Build up the hair.

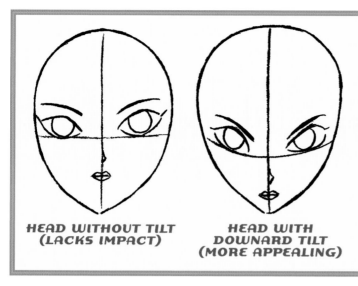

HEAD WITHOUT TILT
(LACKS IMPACT)

HEAD WITH
DOWNARD TILT
(MORE APPEALING)

DRAWING DYNAMIC EYE CONTACT

When drawing a character who is looking directly at the viewer, eye contact is very important. A flat-on look won't do the trick. To create more of a mood, tilt the head down slightly, and have the character look up from under her eyelashes.

Fairies in Flight

Fairies are light, nimble beings. They can be found hovering over a flower, or sometimes above a group of lost hikers, offering to guide them to safety. But when threatened, fairies dash and dart with the quickness of a hummingbird. Therefore, their flying poses must be athletic and streamlined.

The arms are straight, making her pose more streamlined.

Note the gently curving line of the leg.

The skirt trails off, indicating motion.

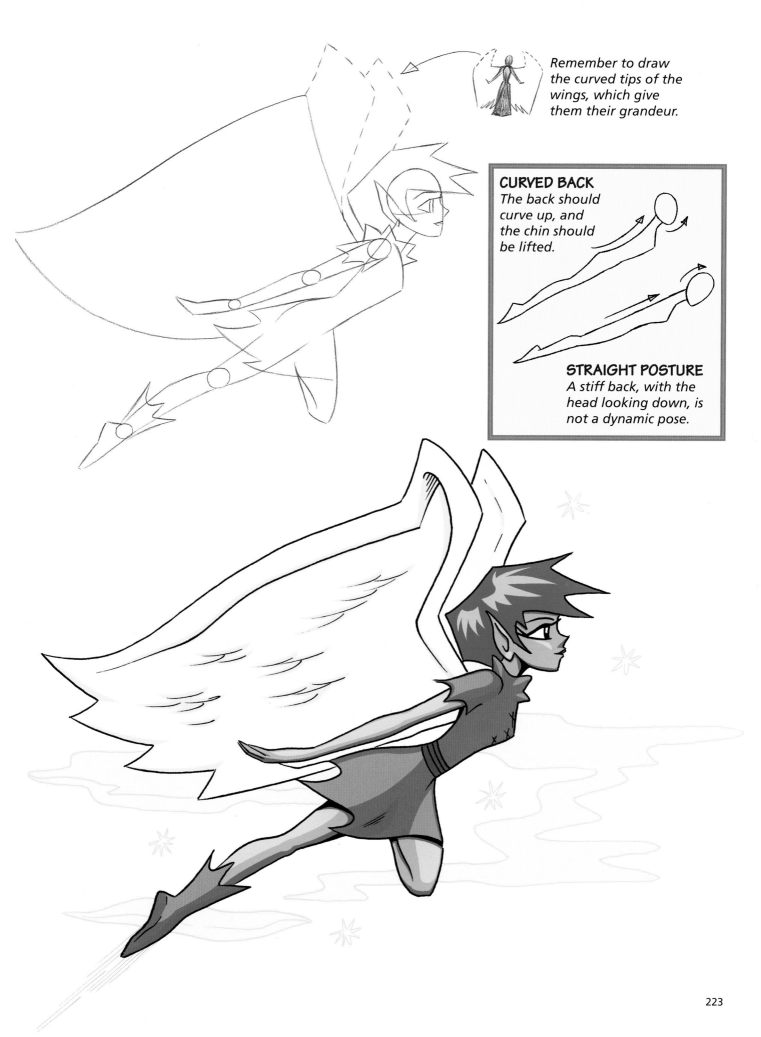

Remember to draw the curved tips of the wings, which give them their grandeur.

CURVED BACK
The back should curve up, and the chin should be lifted.

STRAIGHT POSTURE
A stiff back, with the head looking down, is not a dynamic pose.

MAGICAL EFFECTS!

Magical effects add excitement to a scene and are an important part of the fantasy style. It's really cool to draw lightning bolts and other special effects, but first make sure that your character is well drawn.

See how the front leg looks longer than the back leg, even though we know they are really the same size? The front arm also looks longer than the back one. This is because of *perspective*, an important principle in drawing that says things closer to you will look larger than things that are farther away.

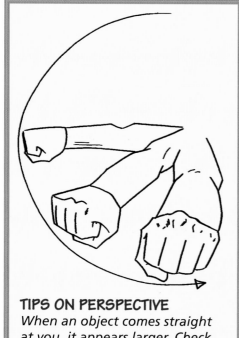

TIPS ON PERSPECTIVE
When an object comes straight at you, it appears larger. Check out how big this fist looks!

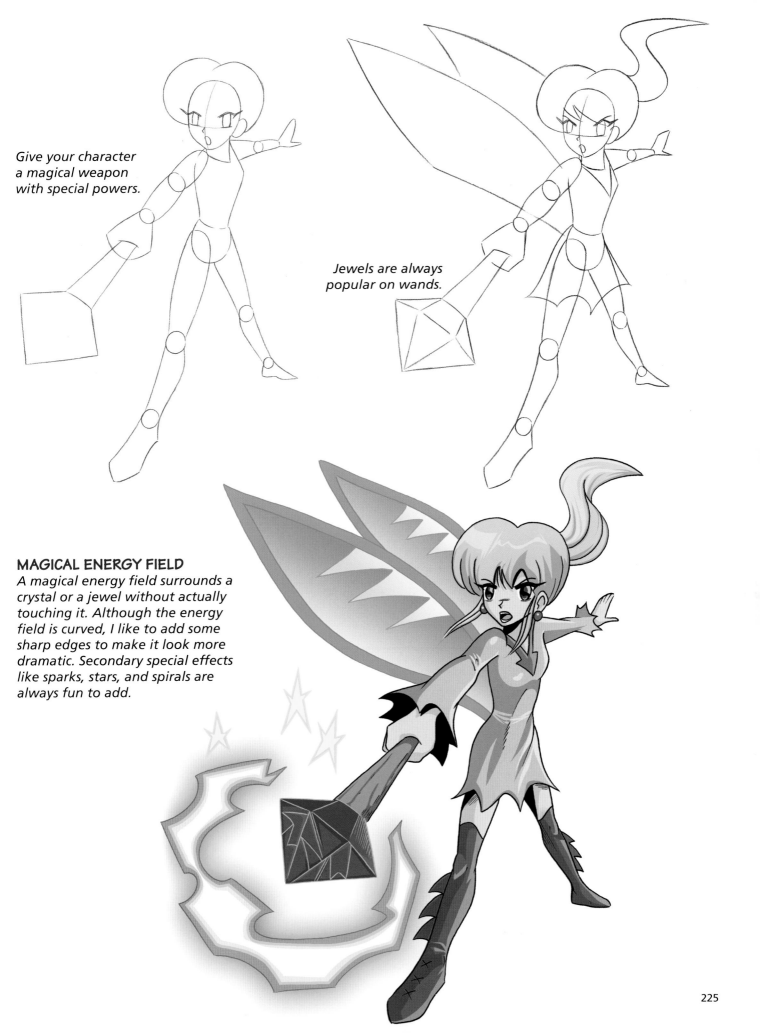

Give your character a magical weapon with special powers.

Jewels are always popular on wands.

MAGICAL ENERGY FIELD

A magical energy field surrounds a crystal or a jewel without actually touching it. Although the energy field is curved, I like to add some sharp edges to make it look more dramatic. Secondary special effects like sparks, stars, and spirals are always fun to add.

Creating Threads of Magic

This enchanted character has the power to conjure magic out of thin air. She can weave together a tapestry of magical forces and use them to cast a spell on an enemy, or call on great forces to assist her when she is in danger.

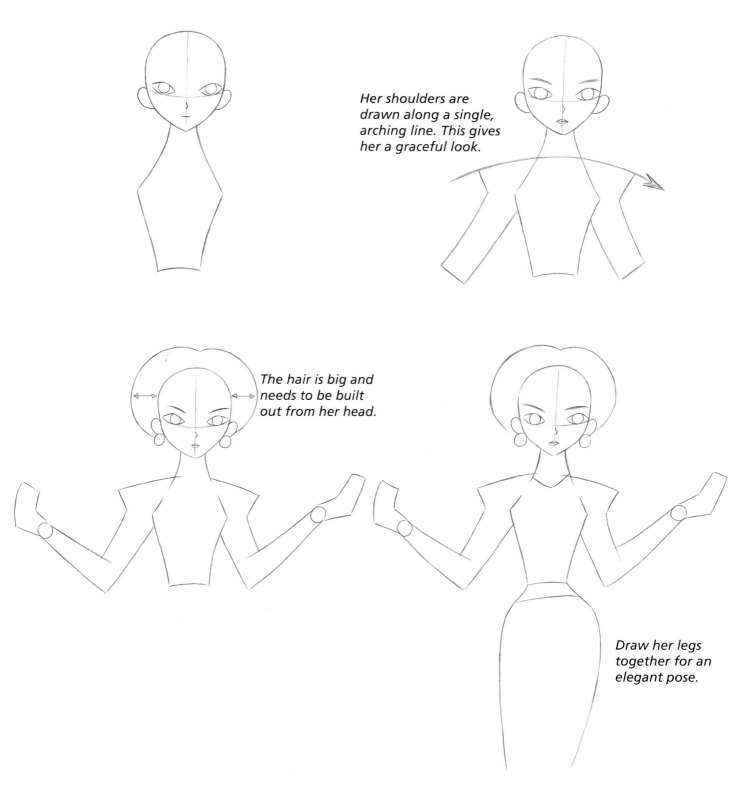

Her shoulders are drawn along a single, arching line. This gives her a graceful look.

The hair is big and needs to be built out from her head.

Draw her legs together for an elegant pose.

TIP
When you build the hair out, making it puffier, be sure to build it out equally in all directions.

She weaves pure magic through her outstretched arms.

Add magical emblems to her costume.

The Magical Staff

In fantasy manga, characters can summon great energies, and harness the forces of nature. With her tall and magical staff, this character is bringing forth a gigantic storm.

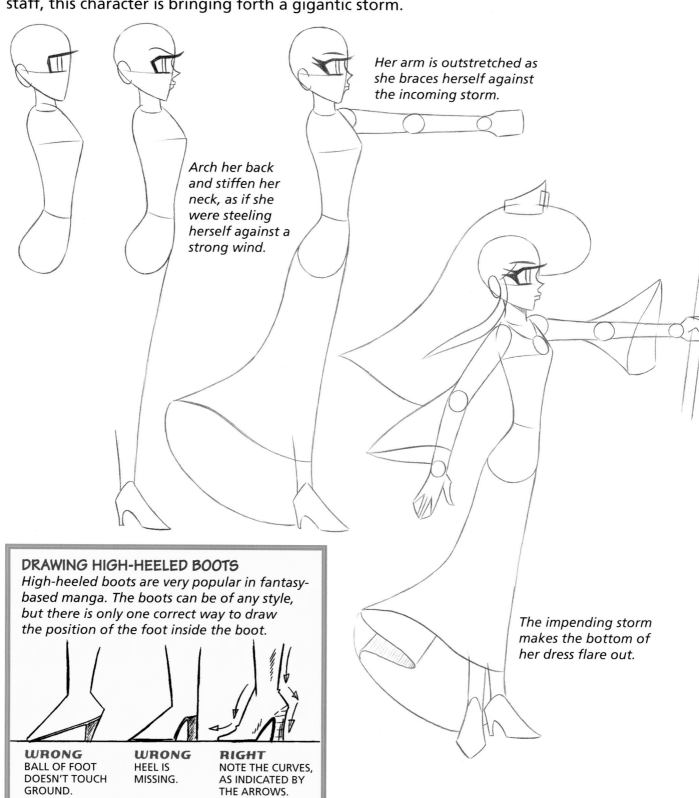

Her arm is outstretched as she braces herself against the incoming storm.

Arch her back and stiffen her neck, as if she were steeling herself against a strong wind.

The impending storm makes the bottom of her dress flare out.

DRAWING HIGH-HEELED BOOTS
High-heeled boots are very popular in fantasy-based manga. The boots can be of any style, but there is only one correct way to draw the position of the foot inside the boot.

WRONG
BALL OF FOOT DOESN'T TOUCH GROUND.

WRONG
HEEL IS MISSING.

RIGHT
NOTE THE CURVES, AS INDICATED BY THE ARROWS.

Magical Weapons

In the fantasy realm, weapons are spectacular and can summon massive amounts of energy from all directions. Although a dazzling weapon is eye-catching, to look brave, your character needs a heroic pose. The higher a knight holds his weapon the more fearless he will look.

WEAK

STRONG

HEROIC

HEAD TURNS

I'm reaching into the vault again. This technique is easy, but it will instantly turn an ordinary pose into a dramatic one. Most people draw the head facing in the same direction as the body. For a more dramatic pose, simply turn the head away from the body.

ONLY OKAY
The pose looks much weaker when his head is facing the same direction as his body.

BETTER!
This cool space guy's body is facing straight ahead, but he is glancing back over his shoulder. He needs to keep an eye on the alien invaders that are chasing him.

Power Packs

High-tech power packs are a cool addition to a whole bunch of characters. Don't be afraid to use futuristic equipment with medieval knights. The fantasy genre of manga is very versatile. Time periods are never kept pure. This adds more excitement to a story. There are many types of power packs.

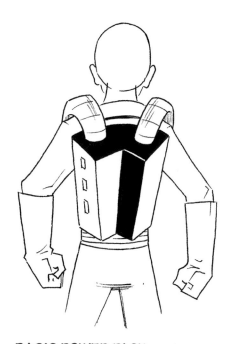

BASIC POWER PACK
This type is used as a reservoir of power, either to give the wearer extra strength or to power up the character's weapons system.

HANDS-FREE POWER PACK
The user can fly and use his arms with this jetpack. This is a great advantage for fight scenes in the air.

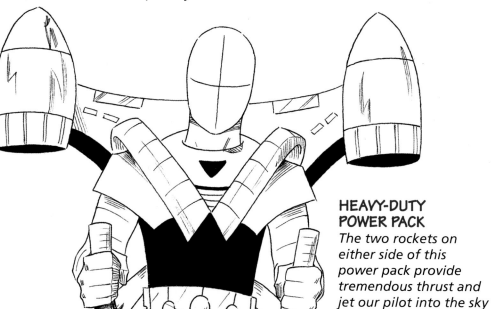

TWO-HANDLED POWER PACK
This kind of backpack provides liftoff power. The bottoms of his boots have jets coming out of them and complete this cool look.

HEAVY-DUTY POWER PACK
The two rockets on either side of this power pack provide tremendous thrust and jet our pilot into the sky at amazing speeds.

SUPERNATURAL BEINGS

The world of fantasy-style manga is filled with imaginative and magical creatures that you won't find anywhere else!

Human-Animal Characters

Catgirls are popular in fantasy manga. These characters are a combination of humans and cats. The posture is totally human. But enough catlike traits are added to create a unique personality. Typically, cat ears, a cat's tail, and paws are added. Sometimes, whiskers and scruffy fur are added, too. But catgirls are always pretty characters, so be careful not to overdo the animal qualities.

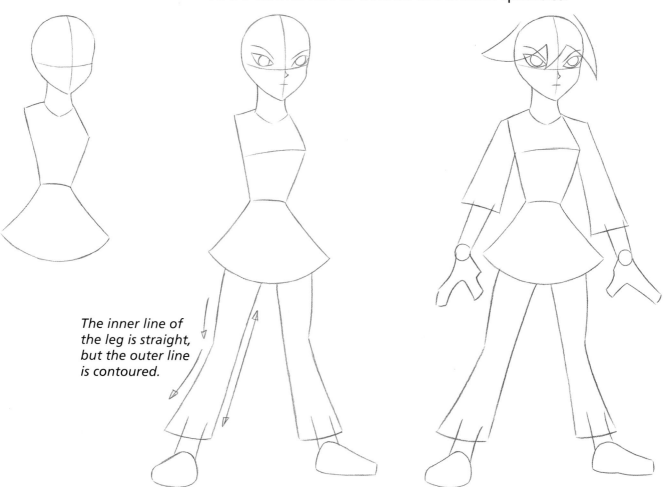

The inner line of the leg is straight, but the outer line is contoured.

A straight tail is awkward. Curl it for better results.

Wizards and Warlocks

Characters in long robes are easy to draw because most of their bodies are covered. The trick is to draw the shoulders extra wide; this will make your character look impressive. Most wizards have full beards and mustaches. They are also usually old, and a bit on the bony and creaky side.

HOW HIGH TO DRAW THE COLLAR
To make a character look more mysterious and powerful, draw a high collar.

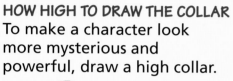

LOW COLLAR
looks weak (collar at chin level)

HIGH COLLAR
looks powerful (collar at ear level)

DRAWING WIZARD HANDS
Just like faces, hands have character, too. Make the hands bony for wizards. You can achieve this look by making all the fingers skinny, but bulging them out at the knuckles.

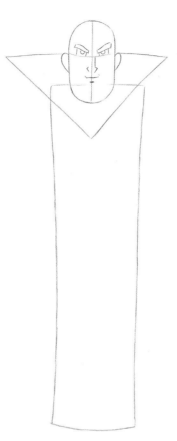

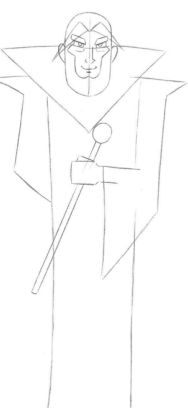

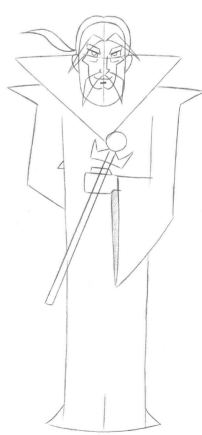

Mermaids of the Deep

These lovely creatures dwell in the sea. Mermaids have the head and body of a woman, but have a fish tail instead of legs. Let's take it step-by-step.

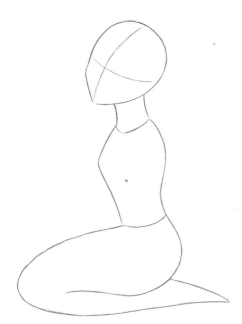

The line separating the human half from the fish half is drawn just below the waist. A slight uptilt of the head gives her a feminine look.

The shoulders add width to the upper body. She has elfin eyes and ears.

Draw two gently sloping lines from the neck to the shoulders. This is called the trapezius muscle. It prevents her shoulders from looking too square.

Remember to draw her tailfin flopping over, as indicated by the dotted line.

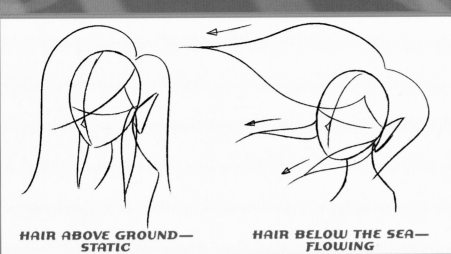

DRAWING UNDERWATER HAIR
To make your character look as if she is underwater, make her hair respond to the ocean currents. This enhances her beauty. The hair should flow gently in one direction as if it were floating. Her hair should be huge, flowing, and beautiful.

HAIR ABOVE GROUND— STATIC

HAIR BELOW THE SEA— FLOWING

Give her some kind of sea-oriented jewelry, like this necklace with a shell on it.

Demon Beast

This super-powered Prince of Darkness is an awesome figure. He should look harsh, with horns and spikes and battle-worn armor. The horns on demon beasts should always be giant-sized: no little "devil horns" for him! His long, draped outfit and shoulder flares let us know that he is the commander. The "V" at the top of his head is a common design in Japanese comics, and adds a cool look.

TYPES OF DEMON HORNS

Here are some other kinds of horns you can draw.

TIPS UP

TIPS OUT

TIPS CURLED AROUND

Mysterious Orb

Not all magical energy is good. Some is evil. Some even saps the strength of a character. This mysterious orb has been sent to find this girl and drain all of her life force. As it glows, it causes her to fall to her knees, which is a sign of weakness. A bent knee pose often conceals the rest of the leg and the foot as well.

ANGER **PAIN**

Eyebrows down are a sign of anger. Eyebrows that go down, but curve back up at the bridge of the nose, are a sign of pain.

PRINCIPLES OF PERSPECTIVE

Characters can look as if they are right up in your face, or as if they are just a spot in the distance—it all depends on the perspective from which you choose to draw them. When drawing your character, curve the horizontal lines (the ones that go from left to right) either up or down to get the right perspective.

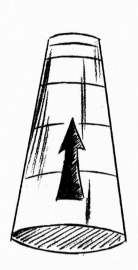

EXAMPLE ON A SIMPLE CYLINDER

We are looking UP at the cylinder above, therefore the horizontal lines must curve DOWN. Conversely, we are looking DOWN at the cylinder below, therefore the horizontal lines must curve UP.

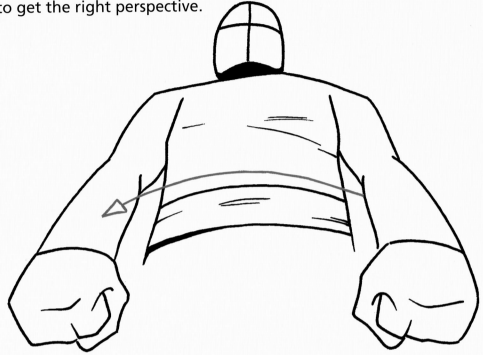

When you want to make a character look really powerful, draw him as if he were standing over us, and we were looking up at him. Draw him big at the bottom and narrower as you go up, and make all the horizontal lines curve down.

If you want to make a puny-looking character, draw him as if you were on the ceiling looking down at him. Draw him big on the top and narrower as you go down, and make all the horizontal lines curve up.

Awesome Character

With massive wings, bulging muscles, and wrists of steel, this awesome character is always ready for action. To make your character look really powerful, remember to use the principles of perspective. Draw him as if he were standing over us, and we were looking up at him. Make him big at the bottom and narrower as you go up.

The Challenge Drawing

This blazing, dramatic scene is an advanced drawing. However, I have broken it down into easy-to-follow steps. Ready to get started? Grab your pencil and saddle up!

CHARGING KNIGHT

Always draw the object a character is sitting on FIRST, before drawing the character. This principle is true whether the character is sitting on a throne, a jet-propelled motorcycle, or a horse.

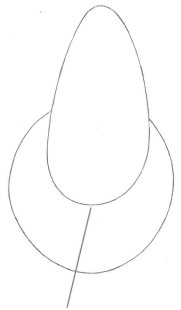

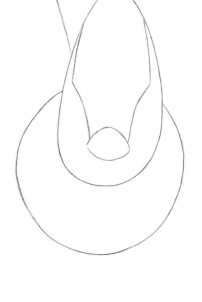

The rider leans to one side so that he can swing his sword freely. (It also helps the picture, because he's not hidden behind the horse's head.)

The horse's chest intersects the neck about halfway up.

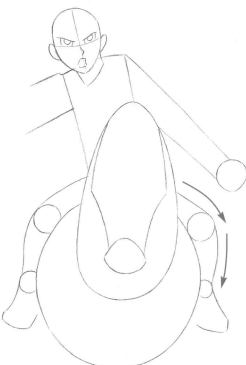

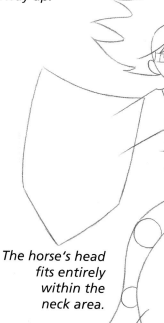

The horse's head fits entirely within the neck area.

His upper legs go out to the knee, then angle down.

NOW IT'S YOUR TURN!

You can use these pages to sketch your favorite characters,
save amazing drawings, or create your own manga scenes.

INDEX

A

Abdomen, 19
Advanced drawings, 56–67
Advanced fantasy-wing workshop, 217
Amphibian hands, 76
Angled horns, 80
Ant-like eyes, 73
Armor, and Bishies, 176–177
Arms, 19
    symmetrical, 58–59
    using as weapons, 50–51
Arms akimbo, use of term, 32
Atomic Bunny, 93
Awesome character, drawing, 244–245

B

Baby-Boltz, 124–125
Baby-face head shape, 71
Backgrounds, 214
Backpack boy character, 160–161
Ball, throwing, 64
Basic manga:
    boy, 24–25
    girl, 26–27
Basic poses, 18
Basic power pack, 232
Battica, 116–117
Battling robots of manga, 48–56
    flying robot soldier, 52–53
    laser fighter, 54–55
    Mr. Colossus, 48–49
    stylish teen, 58–59
Bear-like hands, 76
Belchosaurus, 96
Bent knee, 242
Big circle eyes, 72
Bishies:
    and armor, 176–177
    body, 146–147
    creating characters, 138–139
    front view, 136
    side view, 137
Body, See also Female body; Male body:
    boy, 16
    dividing into sections, 17
    drawing, 16
    girl, 16
Boingster, 122–123
Bows, 155
Boy:
    body, 16
    eye, 10
    head shape, 14

with special powers, 174–175
    uniforms, 153
Butterfly wings, 217
Button eyes, 72

C

Casual teen, 34
Cat-like feet, 77
Catgirls, 234–235
Charging knight, 246–247
Cheerful teen, 155
Chim-Pu pet, 94–95
Chin, 15
    adding shadow below, 25, 27
Chirple, 107
Chubby feet, 77
Chubby monsters, 79
Circle, 85
Circle with extras, 85
Closed eyes, 196
"Confused" mouth position, 12
Crab-like hands, 76
Crabby Cathy, 32
Crabzilla, 88–89
    blackening in the eye mask, 89
    claws, 88
    eyes, 88
Curved back, 223

D

Dark Magic, 60–61
Demigods, 178–179
Demon beast, 240–241
Demon horns, types of, 241
Dino-Crush, 100–101
    leg bones, 101
"Disappointed" mouth position, 12
Dog-like feet, 77
Dot-shaped eyes, 73
Double-circle eyes, 73
Dragonfly wings, 217
Drawing through an object, 213

E

Ear horns, 91
Ears:
    drawing, 15
    fantasy characters, 192
    standing fairy, 207
    super-flared, 80
Elephant-like feet, 77
Elfin queen, 184–185
Extreme perspective, 56–57

Eye contact, 221
Eyebrows, 14, 24, 132, 242
    fantasy characters, 190, 192
Eyes:
    ant-like, 73
    big circle, 72
    boy's, 10
    button, 72
    closed, 196
    Crabzilla, 88
    cute/innocent, 87
    details on, 130
    dot-shaped, 73
    double circles, 73
    drawing, 10–11, 24–25
    fairy princess, 203
    fantasy characters, 190, 192, 196
    girl's, 10
    hypnotic, 87
    placement, 72
    rectangle, 72
    shoujo, 140–141
    sinister, 73
    snake-like, 73
    sneaky monster, 87
    tall, 73
    tall oval, 72

F

Faces in shoujo manga, drawing, 130–133
    front view, 130
    side view, 131
    three-quarter view, 132–133
Fairy:
    and baby, 208–209
    in flight, 222–223
    girls, 182
    hips, 208
    princess, 202–203
    sorcerer, 204–205
    standing, 206–207
    wings, 186–187
Fairy princess, 202–203
    eyes, 203
Fairy sorcerer, 204–205
    and three-quarter view, 204
Fantasy angel, winged, 220–223
Fantasy characters:
    basics, 188–217
    boy faces, 190–191
    eyes, 196
    female body, 200
    girl faces, 192–193

hair, designing, 194
male body, 198–199
natural-looking pose, 201
neck, 197
power fist, 195
Fantasy fighter, 168–169
Fantasy guardian, 218–219
Fantasy knight, 210–211
Fantasy princess, 183
Feet, in shoujo manga, 151
Female body:
fantasy characters, 200
shoujo manga, 142–143
Fizzle Kitty, 92
Flowers, 155
Flowing hem, 178
Flying characters, 216
advanced fantasy-wing workshop, 217
fairies in flight, 222–223
fantasy guardian, 218–219
winged fantasy girl, 220–221
wings, 216
Flying fairy, 186–187
Flying poses:
front pose, arms down, 20
side pose, one arm forward, 21
straight-on pose, arms outstretched, 21
Flying robot soldier, 52–53
Forehead markings, 91
Front view, nose, 13
Funny runner, 31
Fuzzy paws, 76

G
Galaxy ship pilot, 65–67
Gallant knight, 176–177
Girls:
body, 16
eyes, 10
head shape, 14
uniforms, 152
Goddesses, 178, 180–181

H
Hair, 14, 25
building out, 226–227
designing for fantasy characters, 194
fantasy characters, 191
spiky, 194
Hands:
amphibian, 76
baby fairy, 208
bear-like, 76
crab-like, 76
manga monsters, 76
reptilian, 76
robotic, 76
shoujo manga, 150
underside of, 119
wizards, 236
Hands-free power pack, 232
"Happy" mouth position, 12
Head, forward-leaning, 19
Head shape, 14
Head turn, 231
Heavy-duty power pack, 232
Hero girl, 170–171
Hero knight, 42–43, 212–213
High collar, drawing, 236

High-heeled boots, drawing, 228
Hips, 17, 208
Homework Trouble character, 40–41
Horns, angled, 80
Hothead, 110–111
Human-animal characters, 234–235
Hypnotic eyes, 87

I
Insect-like feet, 77
Insect-type head shape, 71
Intergalactic fighters, 173

J
Jaw, 14, 24
size of, 78
Jewelry, fantasy characters, 186
Jewels, 155
Joe Cool, 156

K
Kicking poses, 23
Knees:
bent, 242
of sidewalk racer, 162
Knights:
charging, 246–247
fantasy, 210–211
heroic, 212–213
Knights and castles, 214–215

L
Laser fighter, 54–55
Laser blast, 44
Leader of the Earth rebels, 45
Legs:
number of, on manga monsters, 75
symmetrical, 58–59
Lima-bean head shape, 71
Low collar, drawing, 236
Lunch-break character, 158–159

M
Made-up shapes, 87
Magic sorceress, 46–47
Magical boys, 172
Magical effects, 224–233
creating threads of magic, 226–227
energy field, 225
power packs, 232–233
staff, 228–229
weapons, 230–231
Magical energy field, 225
Magical girls, 164–165
with cape, 166–167
fantasy fighter, 168–169
hero girl, 170–171
Magical staff, 228–229
Magical weapons, 230–231
Male body:
fantasy characters, 198
shoujo manga, 144–145
Manga:
defined, 7
shoujo, 7
Manga business executive, 37
Manga characters, See also Battling robots
of manga:
abdomen, 19

arms, 19
basic manga boy, 24–25
basic manga girl, 26–27
basic poses, 18
basics of, 10–23
body, boys vs. girls, 16
casual teen, 34
chin, 15
Crabby Cathy, 32
dividing the body into sections, 17
ears, 15
eye placement, 72
eyes, 10–11
forward-leaning head, 19
funny runner, 31
head shape, 14
hero knight, 42–43
hips, 17
Homework Trouble character, 40–41
leader of the Earth rebels, 45
magic sorceress, 46–47
manga business executive, 37
manga princess, 33
mouth, 12
mysterious swordsman, 38–39
neck, 19
nose, 13
pointy-haired guy, 28
schoolgirl, 30
shoulder blades, 19
shoulders, 16
teenage defender, 36
top of head, 15
upper body, 16
warrior princess, 35
worried boy, 29
Manga monsters, 68–83, See also Monster
characters
details, adding, 80
drawing imperfections, 83
eyes, cute/innocent, 72
eyes, sneaky monster, 73
feet, 77
hands, 76
head, basic construction of, 70
head shapes, 71
heights of, 74
inventive drawings, 83
jaw size to body size, 78
legs, number of, 75
markings, 81
plumpness/chubbiness of, 79
special powers, 82
Manga princess, 33
Markings, 81
forehead, 91
Mermaids, 238–239
Monster characters, 7, 84–105
Atomic Bunny, 93
Baby-Boltz, 124–125
Battica, 116–117
Belchosaurus, 96
Boingster, 122–123
Chim-Pu pet, 94–95
Chirple, 107
Crabzilla, 88–89
Dino-Crush, 100–101
Fizzle Kitty, 92
Hothead, 110–111

Mousepuff, 102–103
Newmoo, 114–115
Plumpino, 97
Pudge Lord, 118–119
Purtak, 120–121
simple-shape constructions, 84–87
Sneakster, 112–113
Spintop, 104–105
Tailster, 108–109
Triple-Pipps, 90–91
Unibears, 106–107
Wingstar, 126–127
Zot-Zot 3, 98–99
Mousepuff, 102–103
Mouth, drawing, 12
Multiple circles, 86
Mysterious orb, 242
Mysterious swordsman, 38–39

N
Neck, 14, 19
fantasy characters, 197
Nehru jackets, 160–161
Newmoo, 114–115
Nose, drawing, 13

O
Octagon, defined, 52
Oval head shape, 71

P
Perspective, 224
extreme, 56–57
principles of, 243
Pigcycle, 86
Planetary commander, 173
Plumpino, 97
Pointy-haired guy, 28
Poses:
basic, 18
bent knee, 242
flying, 20–21
kicking, 23
natural-looking, 201
punching, 22
Power fist, 195
Power packs, 232–233
Profile view, nose, 13
Pudge Lord, 118–119
Puffy-cheek head shape, 71
Punching pose, 22
Purtak, 120–121
manga lip, 121

R
Ready-to-battle-evil pose, 18
"Really happy" mouth position, 12
Rectangle eyes, 72
Repeating forms, 84
Reptilian hands, 76
Reversed TV head shape, 71
Robotic hands, 76
Ruffled feather wings, 217

S
School comics, 152–163
backpack boy character, 160–161
bows/jewels/flowers, 155
boy's uniforms, 153
cheerful teen, 155
girl's uniforms, 152
Joe Cool, 156
lunch-break character, 158–159
sidewalk-racer character, 162–163
student athlete, 154
teel idol character, 157
Schoolgirl, 30
Seated characters, drawing, 148–149
"Shocked" mouth position, 12
Shoes, shoujo manga, 151
Shoujo manga, 7, 128–187
Bishies, drawing, 136–137, 146–147
boy characters, 135
boy with special powers, 174–175
demigods, 178–179
elfin queen, 184–185
eyes, 140–141
faces, drawing, 130–133
fairy girls, 182
fantasy fighter, 168–169
fantasy princess, 183
feet/shoes, 151
female body, 142–143
flying fairy, 186–187
gallant knight, 176–177
girl characters, 134
hands, 150
hero girl, 170–171
intergalactic fighters, 173
magical boys, 172
magical girls, 164–165
male body, 144–145
planetary commander, 173
seated characters, 148–149
Shoulder blades, 19
Shoulders:
drawing, 16
fairy princess, 183
fantasy princess, 183
Sidewalk-racer character, 162–163
Simple-shape constructions, 80, 84–87
circle, 85
circle with extras, 85
hypnotic eyes, 87
made-up shapes, 87
multiple circles, 86
repeating forms, 84
slithering fright, 87
star, 86
Sinister eyes, 73
Sitting pose, 18
Sketching, 18
Slithering fright, 87
Snake-like eyes, 73
Sneakster, 112–113
Spaceship commander, 62–63
Special powers, boy with, 174–175
Speed lines, 20, 60–61
Spiky hair, 194

Spintop, 104–105
Squashed oval head shape, 71
Standing fairy, 206–207
ear, 207
Star construction, 86
Straight posture, 223
Student athlete, 154
Stump, 77
Stylish girl, 58–59
Superconductive electrical hats/electric
bolts, 91
Supernatural beings, 234–247
awesome character, 244–245
challenge drawing, 246–247
demon beast, 240–241
human-animal characters, 234–235
mermaids, 238–239
mysterious orb, 242
wizards/warlocks, 236–237
"Surprised" mouth position, 12

T
Tailster, 108–109
Tall eyes, 73
Tall oval eyes, 72
Techno-belts, 91
Teen idol character, 157
Teenage defender, 36
Three-quarters view, nose, 13
Throwing a ball, 64
Throwing pose, 18
Tiaras, 183
Top lip, 121
Top of head, 15, 24
Trapezius, 142
Triple-Pipps, 90–91
Turning pose, 18
TV head shape, 71
Two-handled power pack, 232

U
Underwater hair, drawing, 239
Unibears, 106–107
Uniforms, 152–153
Upper body, drawing, 16

V
V-necks, and fantasy characters, 193

W
Walking pose, 18
Wands, jewels on, 225
Warlocks, 236–237
Warrior princess, 35
Webbed feet, 77
Winged fantasy girl, 220–221
Wings, 216–217
Wingstar, 126–127
Wizards, 236–237
hands, 236
Worried boy, 29

Z
Zot-Zot 3, 98–99